T0349627

WHO ATE MY PLANTS?

WHO ATE MY PLANTS?

A Seasonal Guide to Outwitting Garden Pests and Nuisances

Andrew Mikolajski

Michael O'Mara Books Limited

First published in Great Britain in 2024 by
Michael O'Mara Books Limited
9 Lion Yard
Tremadoc Road
London SW4 7NQ

A CIP catalogue record for this book is available from the British Library.

Papers used by Michael O'Mara Books Limited are natural, recyclable products made from wood grown in sustainable forests. The manufacturing processes conform to the environmental regulations of the country of origin.

ISBN: 978-1-78929-660-0 in hardback print format
ISBN: 978-1-78929-663-1 in ebook format

1 2 3 4 5 6 7 8 9 10

Illustrations by Fay Martin
Additional illustrations from Shutterstock.com
Cover illustration by Julyan Bayes
Cover design by Natasha Le Coultre
Designed and typeset by Claire Cater
Printed and bound by CPI Group (UK) Ltd, Croydon, CR0 4YY

www.mombooks.com

For Finetta

CONTENTS

BEFORE WE BEGIN

Garden pests and diseases can be a minefield. Attitudes to their control have transformed over the past few decades and while this isn't by any means a book on organic gardening, such practices are now mainstream and no longer dismissed as the province of beardy types who look as though they don't wash very often.

This book takes you through the gardening year as many problems are seasonal though, since we now tend to manage issues rather than eliminate them entirely, you often have to take preventive action to limit their impact later on. Some pests and diseases are 'host-specific', affecting a single plant or group of closely related plants. Others are less discriminating, seemingly laying waste to anything in their path. As always, you have to pick your battles.

How to use this book

Unlike many other books on this subject that are arranged in a formulaic, prescriptive way, dealing with problems on a one-by-one basis, this book has a more joined-up approach with some problems addressed under a more general topic, such as greenhouses or drought. You also won't find any photos of the pests and diseases discussed, or the damage that signifies their presence. If what you read here suggests you may be suffering from the issue discussed, your go-to search engine will help you find varied, detailed images to corroborate the diagnosis.

Other books on the subject also tend to be larded with cross-references, which I've tried to avoid. I have also steered clear of Latin names wherever possible, as they are off-putting to many and impede the flow of the text. There is a short glossary, which you can use as a gateway to further research on the topic.

Part I:

WHO'S EATING MY PLANTS....?

Chapter 1

WHAT YOU HAVE TO DEAL WITH

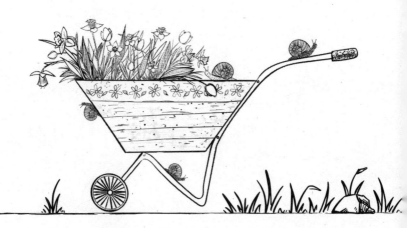

Sometimes you have to wonder why we bother gardening at all. It's supposed to be a relaxing hobby, but in practice it's often anything but. Precious plants get eaten, succumb to horrible diseases, freeze to death in winter or fall victim to sunstroke in summer. You find yourself obsessively checking the weather forecast, and summer holidays are a particular ordeal, when you often have to delegate all your charges to a well-meaning neighbour, and hope they can cope with the responsibility. Pick up any standard reference book on garden pests and diseases and it's like flicking through a medical dictionary – you'll convince yourself you've got every problem going.

Seasoned gardeners get hardened to this. One of the strongest arguments for growing the widest possible range of plants you can, leaving aside the perceived environmental benefits, is that some must surely succeed. Gardening memories tend to be short, and it's easier to overlook your losses when you start planning what you might grow next.

I wouldn't call myself an eco-warrior, but it is best to avoid chemical means of controlling pests and diseases wherever possible. Fewer are available to the amateur gardener these days, and they are much less potent than those used by commercial growers, or even the ones that were available to grandad. But bugs become pests precisely because they're so successful at breeding, so killing a few in your garden won't massively impact their numbers overall – which is what I guiltily tell myself on the occasion I resort to poisons or traps. While a certain amount of damage has to be tolerated in the interests of a  balanced ecosystem, there are steps you can take to minimize this that would satisfy any environmentalist.

Any intervention can have a negative effect as well as a positive one, so you need to balance the outcomes. I like to think in terms of a series of campaigns, and there's usually some collateral damage, either to other plants or to beneficial insects. Sometimes you need to wage a war of attrition.

No two years are ever the same in the garden, and variations in the weather can favour certain pests and diseases or diminish their impact. If you are handy with a spreadsheet (as I am not) or keep a gardening diary, you might like to keep a log of all the plants you grow and the problems you encountered, so you can take steps to avoid the same problem the following year. I confess that my references to such record keeping throughout this book are largely ironic, but if you do have a flair for forward planning and can handle the software, it may be a profitable strategy.

PESTS

Picture the scene. You're sitting under a spreading apple tree in late summer, contemplating your burgeoning crops, and the air is alive with flighted insects. Among the throng, mostly benign, are a few villains. The males have one thing on their mind – to find a mate. The females have two things on their mind – to find a mate and somewhere to lay their eggs. Although they're not overly committed to childcare, they do scope out the local catchment areas to lay where the youngsters will have the best possible start in life. They'll deposit their eggs on fruit tree branches at the very points where next spring's flowers will appear.

There the eggs lie dormant over winter. Come the following spring, the flowers burst forth, the pest eggs hatch, and the emerging larvae crawl their way into the opening flower, causing no immediate damage. Once pollinated in the usual way, the petals are shed and the fruit begins to form with the grub inside it, starting to feed, tunnelling its way round and leaving a trail of excrement. Sometimes the fruit is distorted in shape but as often as not it develops completely normally, to all outward appearances. The grub can nibble its way free, drop to the ground, spin a cocoon and pupate in the leaf litter at the base of the tree, later emerging in full-winged glory to take to the air and repeat the whole cycle.

Picturing the life cycle of garden pests can help you understand how and when you might try to deal with them. Insects on the wing are extremely difficult to control and in themselves may cause little direct damage, but being aware of their activities lets you know that you'll have to deal with the eggs or grubs in the future. This might be a good time to mention pheromone traps, often used by commercial orchards. These are coated with a sticky substance that mimics the scent of the females. Suspended from tree branches, the traps attract the males, which find themselves stuck there. Pheromone traps don't actually control the pest, as while the trapped males die an exquisite, lingering death of sexual frustration, plenty more get lucky. The traps don't significantly impact on their numbers but just indicate that the pest is active in the area, so you'll know to take measures at the appropriate time.

A new generation of products are applied like conventional pesticides that are formulated to kill, but instead deter pests from feeding on a plant's young growth. Some of these are systemic, meaning that they are absorbed by the plant and alter the chemical make-up of the leaves and flowers and are usually applied in late winter, towards the end of the dormant period before the plant comes into leaf. Others coat the leaves and can be sprayed on from spring onwards. The intention behind both is to alter the taste of the leaves and flowers. Pests will still approach the plant and take a bite, but will move on to another plant, with any luck one which can tolerate some damage. The latter type are applied just before or as the pests arrive, and you may need to keep repeating the application as it will get washed off in the rain.

Other strategies include creating physical barriers, so that pests are encouraged to wander off elsewhere. You'll find plenty of these at local allotments, where the quality of crop overrides aesthetic considerations. Plants might be caged, shrouded in horticultural fleece, or surrounded by layers of sand, straw, eggshells or whatever has just been recommended in the weekend gardening supplements.

DISEASES

The number of times I have written that strongly growing plants are largely disease resistant is such that I have almost started to believe it myself (see 'Know your soil' below for more on this). However, plants do get sick; inevitable when you consider that your garden is a veritable plague pit teeming with fungi, bacteria and other microbes – mainly benign, but some very malignant. Once a disease takes hold it can proliferate alarmingly, and some plants are so disease-prone that it's a wonder we still make the effort to grow them. As with pests, prompt action is best, though you usually won't know a plant is sick until it's showing symptoms.

There are various apps that claim to be able to identify plant diseases. In practice, these may not be particularly useful when so many different diseases present similar symptoms, while others look like the physiological disorders discussed below. The apps are of more use to farmers and professional growers who are on the lookout for specific diseases affecting particular crops.

Most plant diseases are caused by bacteria and fungi. Fungi are a fascinating kingdom, more closely allied to animals than plants, and you find them pretty much anywhere. We're all familiar with that tell-tale smell of damp, and wet is unavoidable in any British garden, though its impact varies from year to year, few things being less predictable than the weather. Fungi proliferate in warm, damp conditions, but there are some particularly troublesome types that can multiply even at low temperatures – which is why gardeners hate a mild winter. Yet most fungi are harmless, making no impact on the plants in your garden and co-existing in harmony, like sheep and cows in a field. Some, known as mycorrhizal fungi, are positively beneficial, attaching themselves to roots in an underground network so that the plants can communicate in a mutually supportive way, like a horticultural LinkedIn. But there are several nasties that you are bound to encounter at some point.

Plants don't inhale germs like we do, but bacterial and fungal infections can enter through a plant's natural openings (microscopic valves on the leaf surfaces that allow the interchange of oxygen and carbon dioxide) or through wounds inflicted by a passing insect or bird, or by your own pruning. Since many fungal spores are carried in rainfall, pruning is best done during periods of mild, settled weather – when you are most likely to feel like doing it – so the wound will have healed before the next disease-ridden downpour. Viruses can't enter plant tissue directly but are usually introduced into plants on the beaks of birds and mouthparts of insects as they peck and munch, acting as vectors of disease.

There are few reliable fungicides and bactericides now available to gardeners, so you'll have to combine their use with whatever preventive measures are available. There are no fungicides that are routinely recommended for use on edible plants, and even those that can be safely used on ornamentals have limited efficacy. Sadly, there is often no treatment for a virus and a policy of euthanasia is sometimes the only solution. All diseased plant material should be burnt or put in your garden waste bin. Don't compost it, as the pathogens may not be destroyed in the process, so will be able to affect any plants they later come into contact with.

Using chemical products

Garden chemicals are formulated to be 'safe in use' – in other words, you shouldn't need to wear gloves or a mask when handling them. There's been a general move away from such toxins, and they alter the natural ecosystem of the garden as they kill beneficial organisms as well as pests. Organic pesticides are best for the environment, but such is their limited potency that you may need several campaigns to fully eliminate any pest. There are few garden fungicides available that deal directly with plant diseases and none at all that are recommended for food plants. To minimize the risk of disease, look for varieties that have proven resistance.

To maximize the effectiveness of any garden chemical, switch brands frequently. Pests and diseases can rapidly become resistant to a particular product, so trying another brand with a slightly different formulation, even though the active ingredients may be the same, can raise your chances of success.

PHYSIOLOGICAL DISORDERS

These problems are often self inflicted, though they can also arise from acts of God. Essentially, they occur when something about the growing conditions isn't quite right – usually down to unseasonable weather or some deficiency in the soil. Diagnosis can be tricky, as symptoms of a physiological disorder look exactly like many diseases. To compound the problem, plants suffering from a physiological disorder are weakened by it, and then become susceptible to disease. In the case of an act of God, such as storm damage, drought or flooding, there's usually not a lot you can do in its immediate wake, and such events often occur at short notice, although you can take steps to minimize further damage. However, many other factors that are within your control can result in leaf spotting or leaf drop, flowers not opening properly, fruits failing to form, or plants dying outright, if you don't take preventive measures.

One of the commonest physiological disorders is gumming, though mercifully this is mostly limited to plum trees. Beads of viscous, translucent, amber-like jelly can be seen oozing from the bark, and on, or even inside, the fruits. There's no specific cause other than a sudden weather change that's put a check on the plant's growth – a hard frost, prolonged drought, strong winds or simply exhaustion from coping with the burden of a heavy crop.

Plants can suffer from stress just like we do. Sometimes it can be alleviated, sometimes not.

Know your soil

Did your heart just sink, reading that heading? I understand that this is an impossible ask. You cannot form any detailed assessment of your soil just by looking at it and, as its mineral content is likely to vary across the garden, it's pointless to attempt any kind of thorough chemical analysis, as you can only ever test a tiny sample. Potential deficiencies that might affect how your plants grow are difficult to identify until the evidence of yellowing or spotty leaves is visible, and even then precise diagnosis can be tricky. Yet soil structure, which also has an impact on plant health, is easy to assess and there's a simple test that will impress your novice gardener pals. Reach down and gather up a handful of soil, then squeeze it in your hand. Ideally, you'll be able to rub the soil through your fingers to form nice damp crumbs that leave your hands more or less clean, like when you make pastry. That's 'friable loam', the holy grail of gardening that nearly all plants will thrive in. If the soil feels dry and won't bind but runs through your fingers, chances are it has a high sand content and the plants will likely have a starved, stretched look about them because water drains through it so swiftly. Come to my Northamptonshire garden, and you'd be able to squeeze the handful of soil into a damp sausage – I'm on clay, so there's often too much water in the soil and that permanent dampness around the roots means they grow lushly, with the excessively soft growth being particularly susceptible to disease. You can bring both the latter two types closer to the ideal – and thus reduce the risk of plant problems – by liberal applications of compost.

Ah yes, compost – something else to stress about. In summer, a compost heap is supposed to break down into a sweet-smelling, crumbly material, generating considerable heat (by the action of beneficial bacteria) as it does so. You can encourage this by regular turning, and some sealed compost bins are designed to rotate. If you have an open heap, as I do, you can achieve the same result by turning it with a garden fork – as I don't. While an unturned heap like mine tends to get a bit claggy as each fresh layer compresses what's underneath and closes up the air pockets that allow the bacteria to multiply, it's a backbreaking job to fork it through. The last time I did, I nearly impaled a bright green frog, cooling off in the slimy depths I was aiming to aerate. Hence I now leave it alone, and the good news is that material that fails to break down properly can still be used for soil improvement. Just spread it over the soil surface in autumn. You don't have to fork it in, just distribute it around plants, and the earthworms will do all the work for you over winter, by dragging it underground, aerating the soil through their tunnelling, ingesting it and creating a friable mixture in the process. A healthy worm population is a sure indicator of fertile, nutrient-rich soil that ensures plant health. The best time to apply the compost is after a shower of rain, so it binds with the soil, and it shouldn't touch the stems of any woody plants in case it causes rotting, but I wouldn't be too fussed over this. If you don't have a compost heap, or have a new garden, you can buy bags of soil improver which do the same job. You can also boost the mineral content of your soil by sprinkling it with volcanic rock dust, which can also be used as compost activator.

However, when a plant shows signs the soil doesn't quite suit it, and it starts to fail, the solution is often to turn the problem on its head. Instead of trying to alter the soil, dig up the plant and grow something else that it does suit.

Green manures

A green manure is not the result of a dodgy kebab but a non-edible crop grown on a bare bit of soil, usually over winter though they can be planted at other times as well, to provide cover and help prevent soil erosion. After a few months' growth, the 'manure' is dug into the soil to increase the nutrient content of the soil prior to sowing or planting out the new season's crop. However, depending on the type of plant, it can also attract and harbour certain pests. Some are mustards, which belong to the brassica family, so should not be used where you are planning to grow cabbages or other brassicas, since growing them can increase the risk of clubroot.

Waterlogging

Or, more specifically, waterlogged soil. You'll know if this is a problem, as any grass will feel squelchy underfoot and after a heavy rain your garden will become a quagmire, with puddles that refuse to drain. If you're viewing a property to buy, look closely at the soil in the borders: a greenish film on the surface and patches of moss (also to be seen on lawns) are sure indicators of poor drainage. Soils with a high clay content often drain poorly and there are a number of strategies for dealing with it. One is to embrace it and grow plants ('bog plants') that will thrive in moist, heavy soil. Another is to make frequent applications of organic matter, such as garden compost or horticultural grit, to improve the drainage. Clay soils that are wet for most of the year can dry out alarmingly and crack during a summer drought, which is also best dealt with by applying organic matter.

If the waterlogging is temporary and normal service is resumed in good time, many plants will be fine. However, if a period of heavy rain in winter is followed by a hard frost, water will freeze around the plant roots and you can expect to suffer some losses.

If the house has been built on a flood plain or if there is a high water table, installing land drains to drain permanently wet soil is expensive and may not succeed in the longer term if the drains accumulate silt. It is simpler to stick to plants that slurp up moisture, such as willows, dogwoods and the already mentioned bog plants. In the veg garden, raised beds will make growing (and harvesting) much easier.

Plants in pots can also suffer waterlogging if the compost doesn't drain freely, and may show signs of distress such as droopy stems and shed leaves. In all probability, the drainage holes have filled up and the easiest remedy is to tip the pot to one side and rootle through them with a short length of cane or bamboo to break up the compost. Some may argue that you risk damaging the roots, but that's better than allowing the plant to continue to sit in stagnant water. To prevent further risk, try top-dressing the plant with grit that will gradually leach down and open up the compost structure.

Routinely adding grit or sand to compost when you're doing any kind of potting can greatly reduce the risk of future waterlogging, as it prevents clumping and improves drainage. Just be sure to avoid any limestone type with lime-hating plants, such as camellias and rhododendrons. You can substitute perlite or vermiculite as a blessedly lightweight alternative if your back isn't up to humping bags of grit or sand.

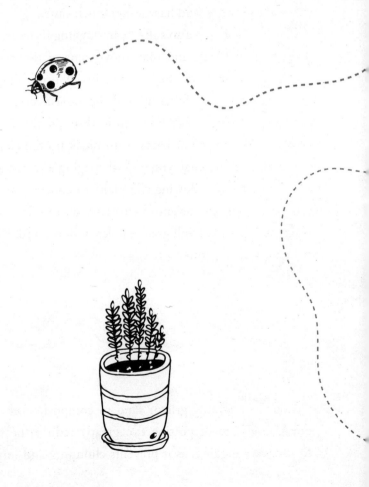

Chapter 2

IT'S A JUNGLE OUT THERE

A mature, established garden is naturally healthy, or so we're led to believe, as a wide variety of wildlife will co-exist in harmony, like Eden. Yet gardens are anything but paradise when you consider the death and destruction inflicted by wildlife in their competition for food. Most pests have natural predators and in order to encourage these, the pests have to be present in sufficient numbers to form a reliable food source. Natural predators merely regulate the pest population, since it's not in their interests to wipe them out so some damage to your plants is inevitable.

To encourage the maximum range of wildlife, you should grow the widest possible range of plants. Alongside this, barrier methods of controlling pests can be effective. These can involve tenting plants in insect-proof fleece (also useful to protect plants from frost in winter) or surrounding them with material that deters the pests. Many pests can be controlled by picking them off by hand and squashing them. You are killing them just as you would be by using chemicals, but you can salve your conscience somewhat by placing the corpses on the bird table, as if enacting a Zoroastrian funeral rite.

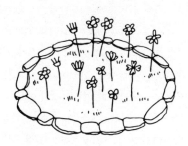

WE'RE ALL ECO-WARRIORS NOW

Some gardeners are seemingly obsessed with using British native plants, but in practice this can be misguided. Yes, British native plants will attract 100 per cent of native wildlife, but your garden will essentially be a planting of weeds. Almost all the garden plants sold in garden centres can be classified as 'near-natives', having their origins in the northern hemisphere. That's a large part of the globe's land mass, comprising not only Europe but much of Asia and the whole of North America. Plants from these areas will satisfy the needs of 90 per cent of indigenous wildlife. And plants from the southern hemisphere (Australasia, South America and southern Africa) have a part to play too, as they often flower towards the end of the year, providing sources of pollen for invertebrate late developers. Aiming to have a plant in flower every day of the year is not a bad policy, and is easier to achieve than you might imagine.

There are calls to plant more trees, and several kinds can be included in even modestly sized gardens. They won't significantly shade out other plants, or the neighbours' garden, and you need the height to provide roosts for birds and bats (and, sadly, squirrels). Think vertically, with one or more trees to give height for the high-flyers, a lower shrub layer, then plenty of perennials and bulbs. Cram them in. Annuals are particularly valuable as they have such a long flowering season to which you can add the so-called tender perennials – salvias, penstemons, verbenas, etc. that aren't fully hardy, but flower right up to the first frosts. Mixing plant types also brings benefits. Your grandad probably grew veg in neat, well-hoed rows, but he was probably also drenching them in chemicals. If you mix the plants up, perhaps even growing some of your veg alongside your ornamentals, you will have far fewer problems with pests. If you do adopt this policy, you can expect the yields of individual plants to be smaller than if grown in the traditional way, the upside being the benefits to the ecosystem.

THINGS YOU THOUGHT WERE PESTS AND AREN'T... AND VICE VERSA

Top of this list must be slugs, now considered a valuable part of any ecosystem, despite the havoc they create in spring. Conversely, butterflies are usually held to be an ornament to the garden, and annual butterfly watches make an attempt to record their numbers, but their offspring can do plenty of damage. Moths are – or should be – as welcome as butterflies, but since they're active at night, you may hardly get to see them. Keep an eye out in April for hornets, which look like turbo-charged wasps but do plants no harm. Also at that time of year, you might come across delightful stag beetles, the males with impressive antler-like jaws. It's worth reporting their presence in your garden to the Wildlife Trust – not because they are pests (they are not) but because their numbers are in decline.

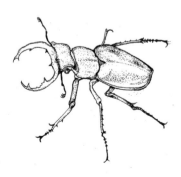

Ants

While ants cause little direct damage to plants, few people have any compunction about killing them. There's something rather unnerving about the way they suddenly appear *en masse*, usually in summer, and since the flighted red ones can also bite, you might find yourself reaching for a kettle of boiling water as soon as you see them scuttling over the paving. But they can cause collateral damage to lawns and border plants by burrowing around the roots, and in this case the boiling water would kill the plants and only a proportion of the ants. There's some anecdotal evidence that ants can be deterred by planting the herb tansy.

Poisons are likely to be effective only in the home and in a greenhouse, where ants can compound the damage caused by other pests. Attracted by the honeydew excreted by mealybugs and the like, they transfer the pest's eggs to other plants while ferrying the sweet sticky substance back to their nests as food for their young.

Birds

Birds can hardly be considered pests when you consider what a good job they do of gathering up all manner of grubs in spring to pour down the gullets of their ravenous chicks. Unfortunately they are also partial to tender flower and leaf buds, and can devour entire crops of soft fruits. If this is a problem, it could be worth investing in a fruit cage big enough to stand up and move around in. Tenting individual plants to keep birds off is not such a good idea, as it will also keep out much-needed pollinators.

Gotta love that slug!

Slugs are the gardener's friend.

Yes, you read that right. No longer classified as pests by the Royal Horticultural Society (RHS), slugs are a valuable part of a garden's ecosystem. Leaving aside what a gourmet treat they are to frogs, toads and birds, at times they are positively welcome to gardeners. In autumn, they do a good job of hoovering up the decaying plant material accumulating around plants that not only harbours disease but can shelter other pests and their eggs over winter.

Not all slugs are equal, of course. The big orangey-brown ones that seem to emerge from nowhere after a shower of rain are the ones you should embrace. Far less desirable are the little black ones (and all sizes in between) that you may spot in springtime, when they can demolish a tray of seedlings in one sitting. In fact, there's hardly any plant they wouldn't attack. In summer, if you move your pots around, you'll see them clustered underneath, sheltering from the heat. Such is the damage they cause that extensive treatment is warranted.

There are various ways of dealing with slugs, but you need to start early, before plants are completely ruined for the season. You have two options: kill them or create barriers that deter them.

Assuming you're of the Genghis Khan mindset, you can still buy poisonous slug pellets. These are now based on iron ('ferrous'), supposedly less toxic to other wildlife than the metaldehyde ones that were withdrawn in 2020 and technically illegal stocks of which you may find in your dad's shed. Nevertheless, indiscriminate use results in a mass of

slimy corpses around your plants. If you can clear this with your conscience – and who am I to judge, as I have been known to use them myself? – then the following is the most aesthetically pleasing way of using them. Instead of scattering them over the soil surface, place a few (four or five is plenty) in the bottom of a glass jar. By far the best for this purpose are the tall, slim jars olives come in, but an ordinary jam jar will do. Lay the jar on its side on the ground adjacent to any vulnerable plants.

Lured by the scent of the pellets, the slugs smarm their way to the base of the jar, where they gorge and die – out of reach of birds, hedgehogs and, if you use the narrow kind, frogs and toads. Then it is simply a matter of emptying the gory contents or discarding the whole thing. The beauty of this method is that the poison never comes into contact with the soil, so there is no chance of it entering the food chain that way either. The best day to begin your campaign is February 14, as a re-enactment of the St Valentine's day massacre, even if the ground is frozen and the plants you are trying to protect, such as hostas, daylilies and delphiniums, are not showing above ground. The slugs are already breeding underground, and if you deal with them now, you have solved your problem for the whole season. This is possibly the best way of dealing with the slugs that destroy your potatoes underground, as the pellets lure them to the surface, though you can also dispatch them using a parasitic nematode that can be distributed by watering around the plants.

Some gardeners get hooked on using beer traps, which you can buy, though a saucer or jar of beer sunk in the soil works just as well. Slugs wander into these – the beer does not attract them – where they die an inebriated death.

More humane methods of controlling slugs involve physical barriers that deter the slugs, which glide off to cause less serious damage elsewhere. One of the most effective is a garlic wash. The following recipe is taken from the Sienna Hostas website (they regularly win gold medals at RHS shows, where use of pesticides is prohibited). Take two heads of garlic (the whole thing, not broken up or peeled) and boil them in two litres of water until they disintegrate. Once cooled, mash the garlic in the remaining water, then strain it and store in the fridge. To apply, dilute two tablespoons in five litres of water (a standard watering can), then sprinkle this directly over your vulnerable plants, aiming to coat the leaves. You have to apply the wash weekly, and renew applications after rain, but it does work.

As with contraception, barrier methods of slug control can be effective without being foolproof. There's a product called 'Slug Gone' – pelleted sheep's wool that looks like something you'd give the cat, but smells more like what you'd find in the litter tray. This needs to be spread around plants in a ring. Once wetted by rain, the pellets swell up to form a fuzzy mat that the slugs cannot negotiate. Over time, the mat will be absorbed into the soil, so you need to repeat applications periodically. If you garden in a rural area or go on country walks, you can gather sheep's wool, often caught on barbed wire fences, for the same purpose. (You can also collect their droppings, which make an excellent additive to compost.)

Nobody likes tiptoeing on eggshells and slugs are no exception. Circling plants with broken-up shells, sharp, pointy edges upwards, can keep them away. Likewise a barrier of used coffee grounds – though these do need to be applied fresh and replaced regularly, as it's the scent that deters. A circle of playpit sand around plants is a known deterrent, but again this will need frequent replacing. It's the dryness of the material that puts them off. Volcanic rock dust works just as well (being black, it can be difficult to see) and will also raise mineral levels in the soil.

To protect plants in pots, run a length of sticky copper tape around or near the rim. This delivers a shock to the molluscs, who promptly turn tail and flee. Since they have been known to enter pots through the drainage holes and work their way up the compost, a few twists of copper wire (as used by electricians) placed over the holes at planting time have a similar effect.

Snails

Treat as for slugs. Unfortunately, the parasitic nematode may not be effective, as snails are less likely to spend time underground where the nematodes are active. However, if you accidentally stand on one on the path or patio, don't worry about cleaning up the remains – the big slugs, your friends, will soon appear to hoover them up in cannibalistic fashion.

Millipedes

Not to be confused with centipedes, these mainly black, overly-endowed-in-the-leg-department invertebrates spend their lives largely below soil level, attacking the underground parts of many plants including bulbs, potatoes and annuals. They occasionally venture forth to have a nibble at seedlings and strawberry fruits.

Annoyingly, millipedes proliferate in soil with a high organic content, which rather defeats your enriching the soil to promote healthy plants. The damage they cause is likely to be minimal, but they like to work hand in hand with slugs, actually increasing the size of any holes the molluscs have created. Hence, the best advice is to deal with the slugs.

Wasps

You probably have colleagues and neighbours you'd be perfectly happy to have round for an outdoor summer drinks party or barbecue but would never normally invite into the house. So it is with wasps: in the garden – well, just about tolerable; in the house – very unwelcome indeed. Wasps have had a bad press just because they're not bees, the darlings of the garden. It's true they have a tendency to annoy, but all of a sudden we're meant to love them, just as much as slugs.

There are different kinds of wasp, but all of them have a part to play in pest control. Social wasps will eat anything, including certain pests, which they kill and drag off to their nests to feed their young. Solitary wasps are also attentive mothers, but make individual nests in holes in the ground or in crevices in walls in which they can feed their babies on whatever they've caught that day. Presumably, male wasps are dead-beat dads of the first order.

Especially useful to gardeners are the parasitic wasps, which are often used as biological control. The females lay their eggs on the bodies of pests, which they temporarily paralyse. The hatchlings work their way up the pest's anus, eating the less essential body parts first and saving the vital organs till last as a *bonne bouche*, just before they are ready to pupate.

ILLEGAL IMMIGRANTS

Every few years or so there are reports of some exotic spider or other beastie that has been found in someone's weekly shop, imported at the egg stage in a consignment of tropical fruit. They usually die fairly rapidly. More worrying are the pests that arrive as stowaways, not on small boats but in large ones, in containers of nursery stock imported from mainland

Europe (and further afield). There are strict regulations concerning the import of live plant material, but inevitably some nasties make it through. They usually disembark in southern England before making their way north and if they can produce two or more generations in a season, they can rapidly adapt to the UK climate and can even outcompete native pests and their predators. They are usually reported in the gardening press, and if you do come across any, it's worth informing the RHS or Department for Environment, Food and Rural Affairs (DEFRA), who will be aware of the interlopers and tracking their progress.

Twenty years or so ago, much was made of Spanish slugs, introduced as eggs in the compost of imported plants. Leech-like in appearance, and rather bigger than native slugs, these were held to be very nasty indeed, but have now receded in significance. Harlequin ladybirds arrived from Asia in 2004 and are now widespread. As predators of aphids, they perform the same valuable role as the native ladybirds (of which there are around some 40 species), but unfortunately they can outcompete other predators and even cannibalize the natives. Research is ongoing: some of our species are in decline, while others maintain their numbers. Asian hornets, larger than native hornets, arrived in Britain in 2016 and have turned out to be predators of honeybees. Any sightings should be referred to DEFRA.

Oak processionary moth

Of all the migrant pests that have made their way to these shores, this is almost certainly the worst. The good news is that it's very rarely seen in gardens, being an inhabitant of wooded areas; the bad news is that non-gardeners are therefore equally at risk. If you do come across it on a woodland walk, you must report it straight away to the Forestry Commission, as it's classified as a notifiable pest and it's your legal duty to report it.

Its arrival in the UK is a cautionary tale, and illustrates how many previously unknown pests have found their way to our shores. It was first sighted in Kew Gardens, where it had arrived on a consignment of trees imported from the Netherlands. It is easily detected, though the adult moth, active in July and August, is heavily camouflaged against the bark of mature trees. But the larvae, which emerge from overwintered eggs around April, form colonies and spin impressive nests of silk that billow out from tree trunks (mainly oak) or are suspended from branches. The temptation to poke these with a stick is to be resisted at all costs. The larvae rest in the nests during the daytime and feed at night, emerging zombie-like in sinister columns like extras from Fritz Lang's *Metropolis*.

As plant pests go, the damage to trees can be tolerated. But the caterpillars are covered in stiff hairs that are easily shed and toxic to humans, and contact with them can potentially result in anaphylactic shock or even death. If you do see a nest on a tree trunk, take a pic and notify the Forestry Commission immediately. A qualified tree surgeon, wearing the sort of gear generally used for dealing with nuclear fall-out, will remove the nests by hand then treat the area with a flame gun.

Hitherto, this has been a pest of central and southern Europe, where natural predators control their numbers. Unfortunately, these predators are not present in northern Europe. At present, in the UK, the oak processionary moth is found in areas of Greater London, but it can be expected that its range will increase.

Xylella fastidiosa

The very thought of this pathogen strikes terror into the hearts of many a nurseryman, though it has not yet been observed in the UK. In the early 2010s, there were reports of crop failures in olive orchards in several southern European territories, all a result of this ghastly bacterium which kills the terminal shoots of branches before extending to the whole canopy and ultimately causing the death of the tree. The impact on local economies was immense. Previously it had been confined to the Americas, where it affected citrus, coffee and grapes. Then it managed to cross the pond to establish itself in Europe like some expatriate Henry James fortune hunter.

While a hard winter would be sufficient to kill it off, and all the crops mentioned above are grown in warm climates, you'd think we'd be OK in chilly Britain. Except we're not, as the disease can attack such common garden plants as rosemary and lavender, plums and cherries (including the ornamental sorts), blueberries and garden trees such as elms, maples and oaks. (A full list of host plants is maintained by the European Food Safety Authority.)

The bacterium is passed from plant to plant by sap-sucking insects such as leafhoppers. Spread of the disease over longer distances occurs when infected plants are transported, which is presumably how it arrived in Europe in the first place. Symptoms are similar to those of a summer drought, when leaves scorch and die back, sometimes leading to the collapse of the whole plant.

On this basis, it's best to buy only UK-raised plants, where possible. Strict controls on imported plants reduce the risk of the disease entering the country that way but you should be cautious about buying possible host plants online or even at a plant nursery, unless you know their precise country of origin, and be very wary about buying plants abroad and bringing them home in your luggage. If you do suspect a diseased plant, you must contact the Department for Environment, Food and Rural Affairs (DEFRA).

Grey squirrels

Technically, these are not illegal immigrants as they were introduced deliberately to these shores, albeit with scant regard to their potential (and realized) impact. The rascals have proved all too successful and have largely outcompeted the native species in England and Wales. I wouldn't call them cute, but their acrobatics are undeniably impressive as they hurtle through trees and highwire it along telegraph cables. They cause untold problems in gardens, digging up and eating bulbs (or, worse, half-eating them and scattering them across the garden like delinquents) and scratching off the bark of trees and shrubs.

Surrounding bulbs and other plants with chicken wire (but not plastic mesh, which squirrels can gnaw through) may protect them and the guards recommended against rabbits will protect the bark of trees and shrubs. Traps and poisons might kill individual squirrels, but others will take their place.

Ultimately, there's not a great deal you can do.

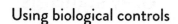

Using biological controls

In the absence of effective or environmentally friendly chemical controls, gardeners are turning increasingly to introducing natural predators of specific pests into the environment. These are sold by mail order rather than in garden centres as they have to be stored under refrigeration. The rub is that the pest has to be already present in sufficient quantity for the predator to feed on (or they will die of starvation), so some damage will already have been done. Nematodes are usually sold as a dry compound that is diluted in water to revivify them, then either sprayed over plants or watered into the soil (or compost) around them. Ladybirds and their larvae are sold fully active, so have to be put to use as quickly as possible.

While they are highly effective, a downside of many biological controls is that they are often active (and hence effective) during specific conditions, with temperature and soil-moisture levels sometimes being critical. Introduced natural predators can be particularly useful to control pests in a greenhouse. As this is a closed environment where plants are often grown in sterile compost rather than garden soil, there isn't the same balance of invertebrate life that you find outdoors.

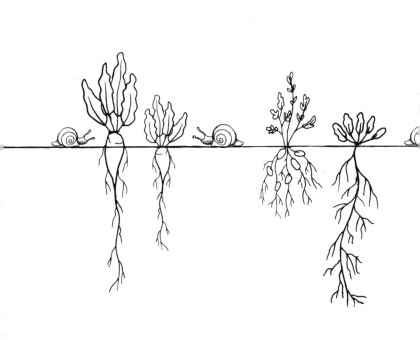

Part II:

...AND WHEN ARE THEY DOING IT?

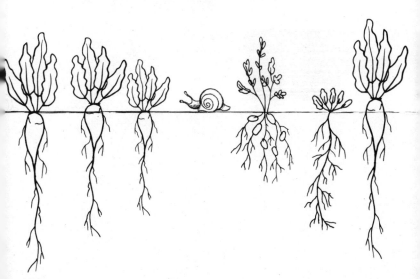

Chapter 3

SPRING

Hasten slowly is the traditional mantra at this time of year. It's a stop-start-go sort of season, when mild sunny weather, which many pests love, alternates with unpleasant cold snaps, which can kill them all off. Spring frosts, reminding you that winter is barely over, are the scourge of gardeners. Air frosts can put paid to fruit tree blossom, camellia and magnolia flowers and the tender young leaves of Japanese maples. A 'blackthorn winter' in April (when blackthorn is flowering abundantly in the hedgerows, at least where I live) with freezing temperatures and even snowfall can throw everything out of kilter.

This is bound to be one of your busiest periods in the garden with plenty of seed-sowing, planting and pruning. It's just as well that this is when your interest in gardening is likely to be at its keenest.

THE DARLING BUGS OF MAY

...And indeed of other spring months. Like a Renaissance explorer, I tend to navigate my way through the gardening year by means of the equinoxes and solstices. Many plants can grow (slowly) and flower from January, once the winter solstice is behind them, but when the hours of daylight exceed the hours of darkness, around March 20, not only does plant growth visibly accelerate, but pests suddenly appear. Plenty of these will have come through the winter as eggs laid the previous summer, or as pupae, often underground.

Aphids

'Aphid' is a generic term covering a vast range of little nasties, including the greenfly that attack your roses. Not all are capable of flight, some flitting about on currents of air, a kind of hang-gliding. They're prolific in spring, when there's plenty of tasty young growth around, and can give birth to live young, skipping that time-consuming egg-hatching business. They can also, later in the year, lay eggs to overwinter and hatch the following spring. A small aphid infestation may cause few problems, but in larger numbers they can weaken plants, making them susceptible to disease.

A healthy ladybird population can help control aphids (they farm them). You can also spray the aphids with an insecticide, or dislodge them with a strong jet of water from the water pistol you also use to deter cats, or a blast from a compressed air aerosol intended for cleaning computer keyboards. I usually rub them off with fingers and thumb. If you don't have any ladybirds, you can buy them online as larvae or adults.

Asparagus beetle

These gourmets among pests attack only asparagus, starting their campaign in May, when the spears are at their most succulent. Since asparagus is a perennial crop generally grown in dedicated raised beds (for good drainage), pest control can be relatively straightforward, as you won't have to scrabble around on all fours. Both adults and larvae attack the plants, with two generations a year. Some adults burrow underground at the end of the season to overwinter and re-emerge the following spring when the crop gets going.

The good news is that the asparagus beetles won't demolish their food source entirely, and they seem to prefer the leaves to the spears, although they do weaken the plants' ability to produce spears in the following year. If they gnaw at the bark of the stems, the upper part, the bit you want to eat, will dry up. Pesticides are available, but the best method of control is to pick off adults and larvae by hand, and if you come across any of the black eggs that they sometimes lay on the spears, wipe them off promptly.

Carrot root fly

This is another instance of the offspring causing all the problems. The adults are small, black, winged creatures active from mid- to late spring. Like fighter pilots, they zoom around close to the ground, stopping to lay eggs on the soil surface. The larvae burrow underground to feed on the carrots, so you won't see any direct damage until harvest time, though a wilting and reddening of the leaves along the way is a sure sign that trouble

is brewing. Unchecked, the larvae pupate into a larger, second generation of adults that will do their laying between July and August and are even deadlier to the later crops. The larvae are also partial to parsnips, celery, celeriac, parsley and coriander.

Attempting to spray flighted insects with a pesticide is pointless, so barrier methods of control are best. A physical screen, some 60 cm high, of polythene or other transparent synthetic material placed around the plants is highly effective, as the flies will dumbly crash into it. (Nip down the allotments and you're bound to come across growers using this foolproof method.) If you have a lawn, you can also cover your crops with a thick but loose mulch of grass clippings, which makes egg laying difficult.

As the scent of the carrots attracts the flies, intercropping (a modern take on traditional crop rotation) by planting them alongside strongly aromatic herbs such as rosemary, sage and wormwood, or more pungent onions and garlic, can dumbfound the pests. Some carrot varieties show some resistance to the fly, so check the seed packets when sowing.

Flea beetles

These are indeed beetles not fleas, but the athletic way they jump about has given them their name. Health fanatics, they're keen on all the foods your kids hate: cabbages, kale, radishes and other brassicas (including related ornamentals such as wallflowers). Both adults and larvae cause damage to plants over a long period in spring and summer, but it's more likely to be critical on young plants and seedlings in spring. They won't destroy an established crop, but will nibble holes in the leaves.

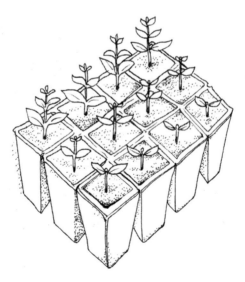

They hate rain, so if it's a wet spring your plants may escape relatively unscathed. Keeping vulnerable young plants well watered during dry weather can help put them off. A fleece of fine mesh spread over seedlings will protect them until they are established and growing strongly, but if you have a heavy infestation there are pesticides available that can help control numbers.

Since adult flea beetles overwinter in plant debris, laying their eggs the following spring, there's an argument for clearing away any dead plant material in autumn from wherever you're planning to grow brassicas the following year.

Gooseberry sawfly

Teenage pregnancy is obviously an issue for these serious pests as they're capable of producing three generations a year, the first brood emerging in late spring, then later ones in mid- and late summer. A serious campaign against the first generation may help reduce the numbers of later progeny, but you'll still need to keep an eye on your plants. While they prefer gooseberries, they'll also have a go at white and red currants, stripping away all the leaves while leaving the fruits intact. Weirdos.

As with other sawflies, the caterpillar-like larvae do all the damage. And while this might be tolerated, if they defoliate the plant they can reduce its overall vigour and thus its ability to fruit the following year.

The adults, emerging from their overwintering cocoons around April, lay their eggs on the undersides of leaves, so this is when you need to start picking them off and squashing them, assuming you're not using one of the few remaining pesticides. Unfortunately, the laying females head for the heart of the plant, where they're difficult to spot, and the larvae start working their way outwards towards the perimeter. This is when you'll be glad you chose a thornless variety of gooseberry. The good news is that affected plants usually recover well, though they may be exhausted from the attack and not crop so well the following year.

Growing your bushes in a fruit cage won't help in tackling this pest. To get ahead of it in autumn, clear away debris from around the base of the plants which may be harbouring its cocoons.

Leatherjackets

These destructive grubs – legless, greyish brown in colour and completely loathsome – are the offspring of the daddy-long-legs you find in the bathroom. Since leatherjackets are mainly active underground, you seldom encounter them directly, the sole clue to their presence being that plants turn yellow and die, the grubs having gnawed at their roots and lower stems. Brown patches on the lawn (and later in summer) can also indicate they are active, and they occasionally come to the surface. In borders, there's no control other than a parasitic nematode, *Steinernema feltiae*, but this is only active at warm temperatures so is really only effective when applied in summer (when it can also be used on lawns). You can expect more leatherjackets if the previous autumn was a particularly wet one, so make a note of this in your gardening diary.

If you think you have a problem among your border plants, the only reasonable remedy in spring is to get on your hands and knees and with a hand fork loosen the soil around any of them that appear affected. You may come across the grubs, which you can then destroy or feed to the birds. On a lawn, water where you think they are active, then cover with black plastic (a cut-up empty compost bag would be ideal for this) – the dampness will encourage the grubs to come to the surface overnight. The following day, you can remove the plastic and dispose of the grubs as you see fit. If you are literally up with the lark, you might just remove the plastic and expose them to the ravenous early birds that will pick them off for you.

Leek moth

The caterpillars of this moth must have the worst breath of any garden pest, as they seem to survive on a diet of not only leeks but the related onions, chives, garlic and shallots. Fail to get on top of them in May to June and you'll be landed with a second generation in August to October. The adults of the second generation can overwinter in plant debris (an argument for an autumn clear-up, if you had a serious infestation) and lay their eggs the following spring.

The larvae tunnel into precisely the parts of the plant you want to eat yourself. If you've had a spring infestation (which you won't know about till you harvest), you may see silky cocoons on the upper parts of the plants that you can pick off and crush, avoiding further damage to later crops. The tunnelling may not be extensive, and you can still end up with a decent crop. Since there's no available insecticide, you can strategically delay sowing till June (or even later) to avoid the first generation entirely. Or grow the whole crop under insect-proof fleece to keep the adult moths out completely.

This pest is mainly active in the balmy south of England, but it is spreading northwards.

Lily beetle

Lilies have gone out of fashion somewhat. Bare bulbs used to be routinely available in garden centres around November (the best time for planting), but now they're generally sold around spring, alongside dahlias and gladioli. The reason for their fall from grace is the lily beetle, a pest that used to be confined to warmer regions but is now found virtually anywhere. Most gardeners are aware that lilies are toxic to cats, another reason for their fall from grace. Cats don't eat the plants, but the pollen clings to their fur and gets into their stomachs when they wash themselves, causing kidney problems. If you don't have cats, or figure they can take their chances, the scent of lilies, heady and complex, is enough justification for growing them. But you must be on your guard against lily beetle, which can ruin the display, probably to the great entertainment of the cats.

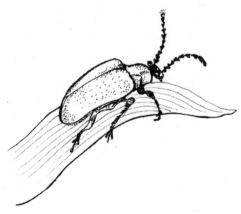

At first glance, a lily beetle is a handsome thing, a brilliant scarlet creature that is hard to miss. Strangely, they are unpalatable to birds, who give them a wide berth and do nothing to help in controlling them. Once your lilies are well above ground, you'll easily spot the beetles on the upper surfaces of the leaves and often found in pairs, one on top of the other, looking like a London bus. While you can apply a pesticide at this stage, it's simpler to pick them off and squash them.

Do this and you've only done half the job, however. You must then scrupulously examine the undersides of the leaves and thumb away any eggs, which are clearly visible. The parents don't stick around to care for the larvae, who, if allowed to hatch, will crawl all over the plant, eating leaves and flower buds and covering themselves in their own excrement. Removing them by hand is anything but savoury, so it's best to get ahead of the game by dealing with the adults. Hence I now grow my lilies exclusively in pots, which makes control much easier as you can inspect them from all sides without trampling other plants.

This is a host-specific pest – it attacks only lilies. But if there's a mild spring, it sometimes emerges early from its hibernation and is found on crown imperials, which it considers a kind of appetizer.

Pea and bean weevil

Another pest with specific dietary requirements, this weevil thrives on peas, broad beans and the other podded vegetables known collectively as legumes. As with other weevils, the offspring cause more damage than the parents, though this can be tolerated to some extent. The adults can overwinter in plant detritus, emerging with the lengthening days of spring to eat notches from leaf edges, but leaving the crop alone. Unfortunately, the hatchlings that emerge from the eggs the females lay around the base of the plants in early spring tunnel underground to nibble at plant roots, so any young seedlings you pop in at this time can be killed outright. More established plants usually survive the onslaught, albeit with potential reduction in the crop. By around the end of June, the sated larvae are ready to pupate, adult weevils emerging two to three weeks later to eat the leaves of any plants remaining, carrying on until autumn, when they are ready for a good kip. If there aren't any other legumes, they'll wander off in search of sweet peas, so if you grow these for cut flowers or to attract pollinators, keep them well away from your edible legumes.

Control lies in timing your crops, so get that spreadsheet ready. Broad beans can be sown early in the year or even the previous autumn, a time of year when the weevils are dormant. Carefully manage your seedling production in spring, bringing the plants on in pots so they're already vigorous and well-established by the time you come to plant them out. Covering plants with horticultural fleece will prevent the adults from laying their eggs around them, while consigning all the spent plants to the compost heap at the end of the season will remove their nesting material.

Some gardeners like to grow so-called green manures over winter on bare soil in the veg patch. If you want to do this, steer clear of clovers, which are members of the legume family so will harbour the pest.

Phlox eelworm

These are the scourge of border phlox, those essential plants of the herbaceous border. Phlox eelworms are microscopic creatures that can overwinter in the dormant parts of the plant just under ground, in what's sometimes confusingly called the crown of the plants (not the actual roots). They then work their way up the growing stems, stunting and distorting the growth, sometimes splitting the stems and causing leaves to narrow towards the tip. They're active throughout spring and summer.

There's no treatment, and affected plants should be dug up and burnt to prevent spread. If the roots look vigorous, the good news is that you can propagate new plants from them in autumn, since the eelworms don't venture that far down.

Solomon's seal sawfly

As far as I know, this pest attacks only the Solomon's seal, a plant with a short season, so I have no idea what it does for the rest of the year. If you grow this plant, you may spot the solid black adult sawflies flitting around plants in April. Best policy is to wipe away the eggs, which are clustered on the leaves' lower surfaces. Miss the boat on this and you can pick off the grey grubs individually before they do too much harm. Once they get going, they will skeletonize the whole plant, which weakens it without killing it outright. In my experience, plants unfailingly re-emerge the following spring, so while I do this some years, there are usually more pressing problems elsewhere in the garden.

Viburnum beetle

Insect pests often have a different diet at different life stages. Not so the Viburnum beetle, whose larvae attack plants in late spring, returning as adults to finish off the job in mid- to late summer. The damage has a certain aesthetic appeal as the leaves are nibbled away to resemble lace doilies, but if you can deal with the pest conclusively in spring, you've solved any potential problems later on.

Eggs overwinter on the stems and are difficult to spot. You might be able to pick off individual larvae once you start to notice damage, but this would be impractical on a large plant, particularly one at the back of a border where these shrubs are usually grown. You can spray with an insecticide at this stage if you wish, but summer damage is less bad and the plants usually get over it.

BOXING CLEVER

A precision-clipped box hedge is the ultimate social signifier, bonding gardeners with generations of stately home-dwelling aristos. Unfortunately, a couple of issues have arisen over the past couple of decades that have caused radical rethinks in many a National Trust garden, and while you can still grow the plant, you need to be on the lookout for the following.

Box tree caterpillar is yet to go nationwide, currently prospering in the South-East, though there are reports of it in Northamptonshire and no doubt further north and west as well. The adults breed between April and September, during which time they can produce two to three generations, the later ones pupating in their cocoons over winter to start the first round of damage the following spring. The caterpillars eat the leaves and shoots, leaving a white webbing across the plants, a sure indicator. If you can, pick them off by hand, a task you'll probably have to repeat daily. For a heavy infestation, a parasitic nematode will deal with the pest for you, and pheromone traps can help determine their continuing presence.

A lesser problem is the box sucker, a tiny creature that sucks sap from the young leaves, distorting them into a cup shape. The sucker is also a pest of the equally aristocratic bay. and damage to either is often removed by a spring clipping, so can be tolerated.

Both these pests are much less problematic than box blight. This fungal disease, spreading rapidly during warm, humid weather, causes leaves to turn brown and fall, resulting in unsightly bare patches. These symptoms resemble the dieback caused by the more easily dealt with drought, so before you panic and reach for the fungicide, consider whether this may be the cause. If so, just cut back anything that looks dead. Box, though slow growing, is famously forgiving, and plants can regenerate even if cut right back to the base, though they may take their time.

It's worth knowing the characteristic symptoms of box blight. Apart from the browning and shedding of leaves, you may see black streaks on younger growth and/or white or pink spores on the undersides of the leaves. (The disease is occasionally confused with damage inflicted by the box tree caterpillar.) Like nearly all other fungal diseases, it thrives in damp conditions. You have no control over the weather, but reducing the number of times you clip the plants can help. Regular cutting makes the growth denser, reducing air circulation within the body of the hedge, so leave it a bit shaggy.

The blight is resistant to fungicides, which can only suppress the fungus without killing it. To prevent spread to other plants, clear up any shed leaves that can harbour the fungus and bin them. Any badly affected plant is best dug up and destroyed. Like the caterpillar, box blight first took hold in the south of England and has been steadily tracking north ever since. So virulent has it proved to be that some historic gardens have had to ditch their box hedges entirely, drastically altering their appearance.

OF CABBAGES – AND THINGS

While cabbage root fly and cabbage white butterfly are quite distinct and you'd never mistake one for the other, they attack the same range of plants (brassicas) over a similar time frame and can often be controlled in the same way.

The flies, which look like house flies, will eat not only cabbages but other brassicas such as cauliflowers, broccoli and sprouts, not to mention radishes, swedes and turnips. All that nutrition clearly raises their libido, as they're capable of producing three generations a year, between mid-spring and mid-autumn, the later pupae overwintering in the soil and emerging in spring, making them a constant menace throughout the growing season. It's the maggots that do the harm, nibbling at the roots of leafy crops and tunnelling into radishes and the other roots you would prefer to eat yourself.

Well-established plants can cope reasonably well, but younger transplants and seedlings tend to wilt, grow slowly or be killed outright. You can control the pest with parasitic nematodes, but since eggs are laid on the soil surface, barrier methods can be just as effective. Surround individual plants with squares of cardboard or bits of old carpet – anything that will prevent eggs laid around the base of the plant from coming into contact with the soil. Netting plants with an insect-proof mesh or horticultural fleece will also keep the pests away, but it has to be kept *in situ* for the whole growing season, so weigh or pin it down at the edges. If you do have a problem with this pest, grow a non-brassica in the site the following season (a modest form of crop rotation), so that any pupae that have come through the winter will starve to death in spring.

While butterflies are an ornament to the garden and welcome as pollinators, there are double standards regarding the cabbage white, since its offspring are so very destructive to all types of brassica, not just cabbages.

The adults appear from overwintering chrysalises in spring, and lay their eggs on the undersides of leaves, where the hairy caterpillars tend to remain, so if you spot the butterflies around your plants, that's where you should look. They eat holes in the leaves, and while you might not mind damage to the tough outer leaves you'd be discarding anyway, they can also work their way into the heart of the plant, leaving trails of excrement in their wake. Pesticides and biological controls are available, or you can pick off the eggs and caterpillars as you spot them. More humanely, just tent plants with fleece or insect netting when you plant them out, as you would to prevent cabbage root flies. However, you have to be sure that any covering is not actually in contact with the plants, otherwise the butterflies will cunningly lay their eggs through it. If you drape the fleece over wire hoops, make sure you keep raising the height as the plants grow to avoid this problem.

Since we're supposed to welcome butterflies in the garden, you might like to grow some related ornamentals elsewhere, just as a food source for them. Nasturtiums would be a good choice, though the butterflies will still be drawn to your brassicas.

In summer to autumn, your cabbages and other brassicas may also suffer from clubroot.

KNOW YOUR ONIONS

Onion flies look a lot like ordinary house flies, and they are prolific breeders, producing up to three generations a year. Adult flies emerge around May from pupae overwintered in the soil, laying their eggs on the young leaves of onions, leeks and shallots, or on the soil surface around the plants. The maggots are annoyingly mobile, moving from plant to plant to feed on the roots and the onion bulbs themselves, and can kill seedlings outright. Since they're active underground, the only evidence of their activities will be a yellowing and wilting of the leaves, similar to the effects of drought. Since attacks are worst during dry weather, you may suffer a double whammy if you don't mistake one issue for the other.

There is no available insecticide. Insect-proof netting can be effective, but if you've had a heavy infestation, you can enact a kind of *auto-da-fé* in late summer by digging up all the plants and burning them. That should prevent the maggots from completing their life cycle and destroying next year's crops.

Onion white rot is a problem to be dreaded, affecting not only onions but related plants such as leeks and garlic. This fungus, which can survive in the soil or on plant debris over winter, becomes active in spring, producing black specks and patches of white fluff at the base of the leaves and on the bulbs, and spreading from plant to plant while the soil is still cool and moist, potentially ruining the whole crop.

If the problem does occur, go for broke, digging up affected plants and binning or burning them. Unfortunately, the fungus can persist in the soil for several years even without suitable crops to feed on, so plant other crops in that patch of ground for the foreseeable future before risking onions again (some authorities recommend a minimum seven years, others up to fifteen, with no early release for good behaviour). You can import the disease yourself on infected onion sets (immature onions you can plant to grow larger), so check the source of any you buy. They should be guaranteed disease free.

POTATOES AND THEIR PROBLEMS

Potatoes are a blissfully easy crop – in principle. There's none of that worrisome seed sowing, you just put a tuber in the ground in late winter, then any time from a couple of months later you can enjoy a tasty crop. If mounding up the earth around the stems as they grow – necessary to prevent the spuds near the soil surface turning green and hence inedible – seems too much of a faff, just keep piling on dry straw, available from all good equestrian suppliers. As a lazy gardener, this is much my preferred option, and the straw eventually breaks down, improving the soil in the process. Alas, there are several problems you might encounter. Apart from the inevitable slugs, in your sights should be cutworms, potato cyst eelworms and millipedes. If you have do a problem with millipedes –

possibly because the soil is too rich in organic matter – deal with the slugs first.

Early potatoes are usually planted in late winter, so keep watching the weather and take appropriate action should frost be forecast.

Cutworms (largely a summer problem) may be ubiquitous in your veg plot, but potato cyst eelworms attack only potatoes and the related tomatoes. Eelworms are tiny if not microscopic, so unfortunately you can't identify them by eye and pick them off by hand. They affect the whole plant, which turns yellow from the base up before collapsing. Dig up the plant and you'll see tell-tale cysts on the roots and any potatoes will be small. There's no control for this, but as the eelworms are present in the soil anyway and can build up their numbers given a suitable diet, this is one instance where crop rotation makes sense. Grow them in a different part of the veg plot next year and an unrelated plant where the potatoes were. On the plus side, some potato varieties are known to be resistant, so look out for these when buying.

On the disease front, blackleg and violet root rot can be an issue. There's nothing you can do to prevent blackleg, as it's a bacterial disease that may have been present in the tuber when you planted it. Affected plants turn black then collapse and the underground tubers may also rot and have to be dug up and destroyed. Usually, only individual plants are affected, so the rest of the crop may be fine, but if you're planning on keeping the potatoes in storage for any length of time after digging them up, it's worth chucking out any that look a bit suspect, as the disease can spread among tubers in direct contact with each other. There's a chance the bacterium will live on in the soil, so don't plant spuds in the same ground for a year or two.

Violet root rot is a nasty disease that affects not only potatoes but other root veg such as parsnips, beetroot, turnips and swedes. Above ground, all may look well apart from a yellowing of the leaves, but the potatoes will be covered with a mass of purple threads. As this is a soil-borne disease, you won't be able to grow similar crops in the soil for several years. Asparagus can also fall prey to this, so if you have your asparagus in a dedicated raised bed, you will have to make a new bed for them elsewhere, in soil you know is clean. Other root crops and celery can also be prone to this disease.

Common potato scab, caused by a truly weird organism that isn't properly either a bacterium or a fungus, is often seen on potatoes (even ones you can buy in the supermarkets) and is usually not a major cause of concern, even if the tuber is cracked. You often come across it on crops harvested during or after a hot summer when the soil has dried out. Keeping the soil moist can help you avoid this, and is another argument in favour of using straw as a mulch. However, the issue guaranteed to keep you awake at night is blight.

SPRING DISEASES

Young growth is always more disease resistant, more productive, and more vigorous than the old. Most plants will recover well from spring diseases, as this is when they're growing most strongly. As far as woody plants are concerned, you can usually prune your way out of a problem by cutting off any diseased stems, and the plant should recover well.

Bacterial canker

This is one of those problems, like chlorosis or bitter pit, that may turn out to be less of an issue than you may have originally thought, as some of the symptoms look like gumming. You're most likely to come across it on your plum and cherry trees, less commonly on peaches and apricots. Ornamental flowering cherries can also be at risk. Patches of bark start to die off in mid-spring and then shoots may die back. Amber-like resin may ooze from affected areas. There may also be small holes in the leaves known as shothole – not a typo, and not caused by insects.

There's no treatment short of cutting back any affected

branches. Choose a nice sunny day for this when you're not expecting wet weather, or there's a risk of fungi carried in rainfall entering the plant through the open wound.

Coral spot

The fungus that causes this is carried in rainfall at any time of year. While you should deal with it promptly, spring is a good time if drastic action is needed, as that's when plants are growing most vigorously and can be expected to make a speedy recovery. Small coral pink pustules on stems are the surest sign of infection, and you'll need to check all your fruit bushes carefully for any signs of infection (magnolias, elaeagnus and acers are also susceptible). Cut back any affected stems, which should then be burnt, as the spores will otherwise persist.

If you don't get on top of the problem at the first sign, the disease can spread through the plant and even kill it.

Damping off

Raising your own plants from seed is a worrisome business. Seeing a tray of seeds spring into life gladdens the heart, but that euphoria rapidly turns to anguish when they suddenly collapse and die. This problem, damping off, is not to be confused with the transplant shock that seedlings always experience when you initially prick them out and each time you pot them on as they grow. The fungi that cause damping off proliferate in cool, damp conditions and, once they've struck, there's no way back. Affected plants shouldn't go on the compost heap where the disease can persist, but you might try deep burial of affected plants in the garden as a form of reparation.

Prevention is the only way to go. Wash out pots and seed trays before you start your seed sowing, then use fresh compost, which will be sterile if used fresh from a newly opened bag. If it's been sitting around in an open bag, those pesky spores may already have got in. Incidentally, multi-purpose composts are less than ideal for seed sowing, especially for very fine seed, as their tendency to clump and retain moisture can provide fungi with ideal conditions. If you still want to use these, lighten the texture by mixing in some horticultural sand, perlite or vermiculite, which will improve drainage, otherwise, dedicated seed composts are best to use.

You'll also avoid the risk of damping off by delaying sowing until well into spring. Sow too early, when temperatures are low and days are short, and seedlings will stretch towards the light, making them weak and vulnerable. Sow early only if you have the infrastructure in the form of heated propagators and growing lamps that simulate natural daylight (and deep pockets to pay the electricity bills).

You may well wonder if growing plants from seed is actually worth the effort. To avoid the hassle, you can buy plug plants instead, small plants in a plug of compost sold in garden centres in spring, and also available mail order. You won't have the same choice of varieties, but nor will you end up with the gluts that often result from sowing quantities of seed.

All manner of mildews

The common cold of plants, appearing at virtually any time of year, but mainly from spring onwards. Mildew infections are nearly always associated with dryness of the soil around the roots and dank, stagnant air within the body of the plant above ground. Since the disease-causing spores are carried in rainfall and on air currents, and can overwinter on some plants, there really is no escape.

Downy mildew often takes hold in mid- to late spring on soft-leaved plants, even such reliable performers as hardy geraniums. Small yellow or greyish patches on the upper surfaces of leaves are matched by fuzzy whitish patches on the undersides. Your only option is to shear off affected leaves and burn them. On a positive note, plants usually recover well at this time of year, especially if you give the soil a thorough watering and maybe a decent mulch to prevent further drying out.

Powdery mildew is most likely to strike during summer and early autumn, as cooler nights condense dew on stems and leaves – especially problematic if the growth is dense and the soil has dried out because of drought (which weakens plants so they are more susceptible to disease). Leaves – and sometimes flowers – are spotted with a grey powdery deposit, the fungal spores. If fruits are affected (gooseberries being notoriously prone, though some varieties show a degree of resistance), they can crack and split, opening up the plant

to attack from other fungi. Best to simply cut off affected parts and burn them – the sooner the better, as this disease spreads like wildfire. Some prevention is possible by keeping plants well watered during periods of drought. But it's as well to steer clear of varieties that are prone to mildew (such as some clematis) if it's a problem you've already encountered. Judicious thinning of plant growth during spring and summer can prevent the stems from becoming too congested.

Fungicides can suppress some mildews if applied promptly, but can't cure the disease. If you've had a problem in the veg garden, crop rotation might help to a limited extent.

A galling problem: Forsythia gall

Forsythias have a brief season of glory towards the end of winter after which they are no more than passengers in a border, so you may not notice the presence of galls, which can appear at any time. Nobody knows what causes these roughly rounded, knobbly growths on the stems, but they are nothing to worry about, if unsightly. You're most likely to notice them in winter, when the stems are bare. Stems with galls can be cut back, but do so in winter and you'll lose the flowers – the whole point of the plant. Pruning a forsythia, whether to get rid of the galls or just generally freshen up the plant, is best done as soon as the flowers have finished and the new leaves are starting to emerge in mid-spring.

Hellebore black death

Yes, this is truly the black death of hellebores but fortunately it's host-specific, affecting these plants only. If it falls victim, the whole plant is streaked and mottled with black, including the flowers. The cause is a virus possibly spread by aphids and, as there's no cure, burning is the only solution.

As an aside, nearly all hellebores look a bit tatty at the turn of the year, just before flowering. Some blackening on the leaves is normal after the ravages of winter and it's good practice to cut back the leaves at this time (you can even do this in November to prevent any fungi affecting the leaves being carried through to the following spring).

Chapter 4

SUMMER

This is the season of bounty, when you should expect daily harvests of sunkissed summer fruits, tender young vegetables and armfuls of flowers cut from your borders. Alas, it is frequently also a season of potential plagues. Of pests, that is, if it's a hot one, as rising temperatures trigger their libido and they can reproduce in sufficient numbers to outcompete their natural predators. A prolonged heatwave brings with it the attendant problem of drought, so you can see why gardeners might find their annual holiday away from it all to be the two most stressful weeks of the year.

PESTS OF HIGH SUMMER

Berberis sawfly

This illegal immigrant is a kind of millennium bug, as it didn't occur in British gardens until around 2000. It arrived in the South-East, since when it has been steadily extending its reach. It seems to attack only berberis and the related mahonias. As with the Solomon's seal sawfly, it's the larvae that

cause all the damage, but unlike that pest there are two generations, at either end of summer. They are fast workers, stripping a whole plant seemingly from one day to the next, so you may not be aware of their presence until the damage has been done. But if you do spot the creamy white, black-spotted larvae, pick them off by hand or spray with an insecticide, though you may be fighting a losing battle as they are prolific breeders and voracious feeders.

An affected plant can recover well, even if it's been completely defoliated; cut back the stems, and a good dose of fertilizer and a thorough drenching will help get it on its feet again. If you do encounter the pest, the RHS would like to know, as they are tracking its seemingly inexorable march northwards.

Chafer grubs

Chafer grubs deliver a double whammy. Not only do they cause damage in their own right, but they are so utterly delicious that they attract predators that can cause mayhem in the very act of rounding them up. These larvae of chafer beetles can be active at any time of year, nibbling away at plant roots (which can be enough to kill some annuals outright), and leaving large holes in bulbs and root vegetables. If you have a major problem, they can only be eliminated in summer, as described below.

On the plus side, they're seldom present in sufficient numbers to pose a significant problem, and you may uncover them in spring when you're hoeing off weed seedlings around your plants. In this case, you can leave any you disinter on the soil surface or the bird table as a tasty treat to any passing bird.

They can be more of a problem on a lawn, where they will gnaw roots, causing brown patches to appear. That's borderline acceptable, as you can simply rip away any dead grass and reseed in spring or autumn, but from autumn onwards you may have collateral trouble with foxes, badgers and birds digging up the lawn to get at them. If this has happened late in the year, repair any damage the following spring, then aim to eliminate the pests in summer.

As there's no suitable pesticide available, the surest control option is a pathogenic nematode, *Heterohabditis megidis*, which is only active in warm, damp conditions, so has to be applied around mid-summer after rainfall – both on the lawn and in your borders.

Codling moth

Codling moth caterpillars are those nasty creatures that tunnel into apples, leaving a trail of excrement in their wake. (They are also keen on pears, quinces and walnuts.) Sometimes the caterpillar exits the apple before you pick it, or you may even come across it at the core. Since only a proportion of fruits are likely to be affected, and they are normally shed by the tree prematurely, this might be a pest you can live with.

The adult moths are on the wing in May and you can hang sticky pheromone traps from tree branches to establish their presence. The infant caterpillars start their tunnelling around mid-summer, so if you're planning on using a pesticide, before then would be optimal. Pathogenic nematodes are available to control this pest, but may be of limited effectiveness. They have to be watered or sprayed over the trunk and branches in September to October, and watered into the soil beneath the canopy (to deal with any caterpillars that have already dropped to the ground to pupate). But as this pest has the gift of flight, there's nothing to stop adults from neighbouring gardens homing in on your trees even if you got rid of all your own caterpillars.

Cutworms

This generic term covers the caterpillars of a number of moths. Segmented and around 5 cm in length, they spend the daylight hours just below the soil surface, emerging at night but too idle to crawl into the upper parts of a plant where you'd have a chance of spotting them. They feed on roots and lower stems, which leads to the collapse of the plant. They're particularly fond of potatoes, parsnips and other root crops, though lettuces are also not immune and neither are low-growing ornamentals in the border. Though the adults procreate in summer, you can expect to come across the caterpillars at virtually any time of year.

There are no pesticides for these. Hoeing around plants (often only practical in the veg garden) can bring them to the surface where birds can peck them off, or you can pick them off by hand. Keep the ground well watered during hot weather, as they much prefer dry soil.

Scale insects

As with aphids, umpteen different species come under this name. Clinging to the stems and lower leaf surfaces of a wide range of plants, these immobile pests are all female, capable of producing young without male intervention. They have a youthful heyday as crawlers ('nymphs'), tiny insects that scamper all over plants until they find a nice spot to settle down. There, they live a nun-like existence, forming closed communities clustered on stems and the undersides of leaves, sheltered under a hard carapace. Like mealybugs, they produce honeydew and the attendant sooty mould. Common in greenhouses, hardier types are often found outdoors.

While a minor infestation on established plants can be tolerated, young plants can be severely weakened. When the nymphs emerge around mid-summer they can be tackled with a pesticide, but the outer casing they develop is impermeable to any liquid product. You may be able to pick them off by hand or scrape them off with a knife once they have reached the adult stage. In a greenhouse, the crawlers can appear at any time of year, but for these a biological control can be effective.

ROSES AND THEIR PROBLEMS

A garden without roses would be a sad place, and you can hardly make a garden without them, but there are few more demanding plants. Without intervention, many varieties develop leaf spots, sometimes shed all their leaves, or simply sulk. However, they can be in flower for a long time and it would be a cynic who didn't benefit from sinking their nose into their voluptuous cups of satiny, fragrant petals. Restricting your choice to varieties that are known to be (relatively) disease resistant is not a bad strategy if you're short of the time needed to deal with all the potential issues below. Incidentally, many other members of the rose family (Rosaceae) are susceptible to the diseases and disorders described here. That includes fruit trees such as apples, pears and plums, and ornamentals such as pyracanthas.

Although they are easily dealt with, it's dispiriting to see the unopened buds and stems of your roses covered in greenfly, the bright green aphids that leave behind sticky honeydew. In summer, you'll sometimes see perfectly round notches nibbled from around the edges of the leaves, the work of the benign leaf-cutting bee and definitely not to be confused with the superficially similar damage inflicted by the ghastly vine weevil in autumn.

Leaf spots are all too common, though young plants with small, bright green, polished-looking leaves often seem to be immune, so look out for these when shopping for new plants in summer. Spots can be due to any number of factors, including environmental ones, but the commonly occurring blackspot is caused by a fungus that manifests as ragged-edged blackish purple blotches on the leaves, which themselves sometimes turn yellow. (Even the stems can turn spotty.) This disease can appear as early as spring but tends to be more prevalent in summer. There are a number of sprays available for dealing with this, but you do need to start your campaign early. In fact, drenching plants with an approved fungicide as early as January is a good idea, as this can kill off any spores that have overwintered on the stems, but bear in mind that the fungus will be carried into the garden again in spring rainfall. Once it strikes, remove all affected growth, carry on doing so even into autumn, and burn it. While shed leaves can normally be left around plants and allowed to break down to improve the soil, this is an instance when any diseased material should be routinely removed, as the spores will overwinter on the soil surface to affect plants the following year. There's anecdotal evidence that underplanting roses with salvias ('Amistad' is a must-have plant in any garden) can help combat fungal diseases. These plants contain sulphur, which is released as a natural fungicide as the temperature warms up in summer.

Rose dieback is distressingly common, usually occurring around, or just after, mid-summer, some varieties more susceptible than others. For no apparent reason, the plant starts to shed its leaves: sometimes nearly all of them. Curiously, shoot tips can stay green and any flower buds that have already formed can still open. Dieback is frequently down to exhaustion, as often as not exacerbated by the hot, dry weather that leads to drought. Routinely drenching plants just after the first flush of flowers in early summer can be more important to the plants' overall productivity than an extra dose of rose fertilizer, as is usually recommended around this time. A thick mulch of organic matter after watering will stop the soil drying out excessively in the following weeks, when dieback is most likely to occur. Your repeat-flowering climbers in particular will thank you for this.

Proliferation is an odd problem, occasionally encountered in the classic, older types of rose. A flower seems to develop normally but then the stem grows through the middle of it to produce another bud. The cause is usually a cold spell when the flower was forming (often due to a blackthorn winter) or possibly insect attack. Usually, only a few flowers are affected, so you can rest easy.

Apart from these issues, there's also the phenomenon of rose-sick soil, which you may need to confront when planting new roses. While you can plant roses at any time of year, autumn is much the best time, so look for how to deal with that issue in the Autumn chapter.

TOMATOES AND THEIR PROBLEMS

Most gardeners grow tomatoes. And most gardeners make green tomato chutney from the unripened fruits in October, which festers uneaten on your friends' larder shelves before being consigned to the bin. As relatives of the potato, tomatoes are subject to some of the same soil-borne issues, such as potato cyst eelworm. For this reason, tomato crops are much easier to manage when the plants are grown in containers filled with fresh potting compost (or in growing bags) rather than the soil, in which certain pests and diseases can persist from year to year. Tomatoes grown in a greenhouse will be subject to further issues, discussed below.

A pale mottling on leaf surfaces is evidence of leafhoppers and is only a cause for concern if the damage is extensive, as it can weaken growth and even cause leaves to be shed, though they can also spread viruses. Pesticides can be used, but a healthy ladybird population should keep them under control.

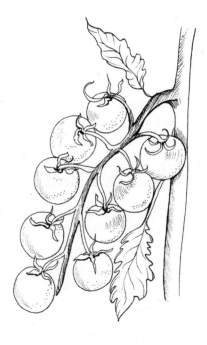

Blossom end rot is one of the most common tomato problems, also occasionally seen on peppers. Despite the name, it's not a disease but a physiological problem. The blossom end of a tomato is directly opposite the stalk. If the skin in that region turns brown and leathery and sinks into the flesh, it's due to irregular watering, which also means the plant is failing to absorb sufficient calcium, essential for cell growth (the same issue that causes bitter pit in apples). Keep your plants regularly watered, especially while the fruits are forming. Strangely, cherry tomatoes, and other small-fruited varieties, are less likely to be affected.

By far the nastiest problem of tomatoes is blight.

GREENHOUSE PROBLEMS

Not everybody has a greenhouse but almost every gardener who does wishes they had a bigger one. Whatever the size, the following pests are almost bound to cause problems. If it's practical, moving some or all of your greenhouse plants outdoors for a spell during summer will expose any pests already on them to their natural predators and the free flow of air and rainfall can help keep them clear of disease. (The same policy can be applied to ornamentals that you grow in a conservatory or as houseplants.)

You won't easily persuade birds and bats to enter a greenhouse and any that do wander in are more likely to freak out than to eat all the pests. So any pest that occurs in a greenhouse tends to proliferate, making whoopee in the humid conditions like when a stag party meets a hen party in Ibiza. On the plus side, since a greenhouse is a closed environment, biological controls can be effective.

It would be perverse to have a greenhouse and not grow tomatoes, which can suffer from all the issues discussed below but others besides, so are dealt with separately and you may have a problem with scale insects, also found outdoors. The damage caused by the pests discussed here is often made much worse by the involvement of ants. Come autumn, you'll need to keep an eye out for vine weevil and the almost inevitable botrytis.

Mealybugs

Not for the first time, the clue's in the name, as these insects appear to be covered with a floury, even fluffy deposit, some of which they leave behind as they crawl around on stems and leaves. (They can also attack plant roots.) The ones found on plants are all female but, unlike the scale insects to which they are related, there are also males. As with scale insects, they weaken plants by sucking their sap, sometimes spreading disease and depositing honeydew, which in turn attracts sooty mould and ants.

Mealybugs can do damage throughout the year but are at their worst in summer. While pesticides are available, these can also damage beneficial insects and call for repeated applications. Ladybirds and parasitic wasps can be introduced as biological controls, but are only active during warm weather from May to September. This is such a difficult pest to get on top of that a heavy infestation often consists in destroying the whole plant then checking over all other plants in the vicinity for signs of the pest.

Red spider mite

This is not an insect but a relative of spiders. The mites are microscopic but spin webs that are more conspicuous than they are. Annoyingly, they've developed resistance to most pesticides but can be controlled by the predatory mite *Phytoseiulus persimilis*. They love it tropical, so keep the temperature down by hosing the greenhouse floor regularly and shading the glass – but you'll be doing this anyway, to prevent leaf scorch.

Whitefly

These tiny, white, moth-like creatures erupt like a cloud if you disturb an infested plant. You sometimes see these outdoors, too, especially on your brassicas, though they're less likely to cause a problem in the open air. The steamy atmosphere in a greenhouse can result in plagues that leave sticky honeydew and the attendant sooty mould everywhere, and they also spread viruses. If they get inside the house, they will light on your houseplants and breed throughout the winter. Pesticides are available, but so quickly do whiteflies breed that they can rapidly become resistant, in which case, biological controls can be effective. Get on top of this pest at an early stage.

Honeydew and sooty mould

It's almost impossible to have one without the other. Honeydew is the shiny, sticky deposit that drips down onto leaf surfaces, excreted mainly by mealybugs and scale insects clinging to stems and the undersides of leaves. In fact, it's one of the first indicators of their presence. (Aphids and whiteflies can also be culprits.) This is a feeding ground for black sooty mould, which reduces light uptake, weakening the plant.

Wiping over the leaves with a damp cloth may be possible, but you also need to deal with the pest. And also with ants, which compound the problem.

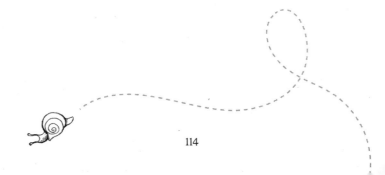

SUMMER DISEASES

Besides the diseases mentioned here, keep your eye on appearances of mildew, which may affect the soft fruits and grapes you're already drooling over.

A blight on both your houses

…to misquote Shakespeare. Blight is the scourge of gardeners, a rampant fungus that affects both potatoes and tomatoes and is always worse in a wet summer. Leaves turn brown and may show signs of mould on the undersides. Tomatoes start to turn brown on the plant and rot. Potatoes can be salvageable if you cut off any affected growth before the whole plant succumbs, but any spores that fall off and land on the soil can come into contact with the tubers when you dig them up, causing rots in storage over winter. Affected potatoes have tell-tale scabbing on the surface and rotting patches in the flesh.

Since there are no longer any reliable fungicides that deal with this and it's a seasonal problem that is always likely in a wet summer, your only hope of preventing your own potato famine is to grow resistant varieties. The same principle applies to tomatoes, though in a greenhouse you may manage to avoid the fungus entirely. Some authorities suggest you should avoid watering your tomatoes from overhead, which would wash any spores down over the whole plant. However, in a greenhouse, you need to spray over the whole plant to aid pollination of the flowers in the absence of pollinating insects. Sometimes, you just cannot win.

Brown rot

Brown rot is an all-too familiar problem on tree fruits. Affected fruits turn brown and can dry out to some extent and shrivel, but the most obvious sign of the problem is creamy beige pustules that appear on the skin, soon covering the whole fruit and, if you don't take action, spreading to others. There's no treatment, short of cutting off and destroying all affected fruits on sight. Sometimes the tree sheds them in disgust, so pick any up from the ground or the pathogen can spread. The fungus is carried on the wind and also by insect pests, entering plants through wounds made by other pests or taking hold on bruised areas of skin.

Fortunately, this disease affects individual fruits only, not the tree itself. If fruits are touching, as they often are on plums (which is what causes skin bruising), disease can spread, and you'll wish you'd thinned the blossoms or fruits at an earlier stage, the simplest method also of dealing with biennial bearing. If that ship has sailed, cut off any affected fruits and burn them.

Expect to come across brown rot on apples, pears, peaches and plums – all members of the rose family, incidentally. If you're planning on storing apples and pears, check them before you do so, or you may end up with storage rots over winter.

Chlorosis

The jaundice of plants. Leaves that should be a lustrous green can turn yellow for any number of reasons: too hot, too dry, too cold, too wet. Leaves often emerge in spring a bright yellow green, deepen to a darker green in summer, then turn yellow in autumn before dropping off, a completely normal cycle. But yellow leaves mid-season, especially on evergreens, can indicate a mineral deficiency rather than a disease, assuming there are no drainage issues.

That may be a lack of iron, magnesium or manganese in the soil – and there's no immediate way of telling. A good dose of a general garden fertilizer and a mulch in spring can balance the soil's mineral content. For a quick solution in summer, try a lawn fertilizer that contains iron (Fe – check the label for this). Iron doesn't feed plants but it does darken the green, so is purely cosmetic, like a fake tan. The plants don't know they're not grass.

If, like me, you garden on limy soil, lime-induced chlorosis is something you have to live with and many plants can also. Skimmias, hydrangeas and *Magnolia grandiflora* can look yellow in the leaf if there is lime in the soil but so long as they grow and flower successfully there is no immediate cause for concern, though again a dose of iron can correct the leaf colour.

Plants that need acid conditions such as camellias, rhododendrons and blueberries will not grow in limy soil. Grown in containers of ericaceous compost, you may still find that the leaves turn yellow and this is almost certainly due to calcium in the water supply. (If the pots are terracotta, the calcium can leach through the pot wall and leave a white deposit on the outer surface – a sure indicator of the water's mineral content.) If you can, water them with rainwater collected in a water butt. If you have to rely on hard water from the tap, it's not worth boiling and cooling it to eliminate the calcium and so long as the leaves aren't actually falling off, it's OK if they're a bit yellow. If it concerns you, watering with sequestered iron can restore the correct mineral balance and darken the green.

Turning this on its head, the leaves of some plants are actually meant to be yellow (such as *Choisya* 'Sundance' and the hosta 'Sum and Substance'). If these turn green, they're not getting enough sunlight to brighten the colour. Relocate them if necessary.

Clematis wilt

That clematis you so lovingly planted seems to be growing vigorously, maybe even producing a few flower buds, only to start to collapse from the top down. The cause is probably a fungus and is not to be confused with simple neglect, or with downy mildew, which is also likely to strike any time from mid-summer onwards. The only solution is to cut back affected stems – probably all of them – and burn them.

Never give up on a clematis. They can take time to get their roots down and get properly going. Even if a plant did very little the first year, they can surprise you in later years. Some varieties seem to be more prone to wilt than others.

Clubroot

This is a disease of brassicas – cabbages, caulis, broccoli, etc. – including ornamentals such as wallflowers and annual stocks. It's caused by a weird organism that isn't quite a slime mould (as if that wouldn't be bad enough) that lives underground, attacking and distorting roots so the parts of the plant above ground wilt and are often stunted. It thrives in warm, moist conditions, so watch out for it from around mid-summer

onwards. In dry summers, the spores might not germinate and you can escape the problem entirely.

There's no chemical control for this, so you have to cope with it. Since it can persist in the soil for twenty years or more, you'll have to give up growing brassicas in the same patch of soil and be wary of inadvertently transferring the disease on garden tools and even the soles of your boots. Practising crop rotation can reduce the risk of the disease spreading. If you buy plug plants in spring, check that they're guaranteed disease free and be cautious about buying brassica plants raised by enthusiastic allotment holders at a local plant fair. With the best will in the world, this is a disease that can easily be spread unwittingly.

If you've ever wondered what those boxes of lime, an

alkaline material, are for, it's to deal with this problem. Lowering the acidity of the soil reduces the risk of clubroot (though does not eliminate it). Some vegetable varieties have known resistance, though none is truly immune.

Leek rust

A problem from mid-summer into autumn, when conditions become progressively damper and favour certain fungi, one of which causes orange pustules to appear on the outer leaves of your leeks. It's a common disease, and if only the outer leaves are affected you can relax, but badly stricken plants need burning. As the spores are carried in wind currents, there's not a great deal you can do to prevent it occurring, short of the usual strategies of keeping plants well spaced and routine soil improvement to facilitate drainage. Some varieties are more resistant than others. If you've had a problem, make a note on the spreadsheet to try a different one next year. Crop rotation can help, too. No two years are ever the same and you may well escape the problem if the tail end of the season is dry and warm.

Go easy on the nitrogenous fertilizers in spring, as the lush growth these encourage is particularly susceptible to disease later on.

Pear rust

This problem is not particularly common, but it is so bizarre that it deserves detailed treatment.

Essentially, the fungus that produces the rust needs two hosts, a pear and a juniper, to complete its life cycle. Junipers are grown as ornamentals and the berries offer a delightful tang to casseroles and pâtés (as well as being essential in the production of gin). Strangely, pears and junipers are not even closely related, and how the fungus evolved to be dependent on both is one of nature's cunning tricks. The problem first appears as orange spots on the surface of pear leaves in spring and summer. Spores from these blow onto junipers, on the stems of which galls appear, in turn producing gelatinous spore masses the following spring. Juniper stems can be distorted and even die back. Spores are then blown back onto the pears to start the process all over again.

So – worse for the juniper than the pear, at least in the UK. In Europe, pear branches can also develop cankers, which can affect the tree's health overall. Perhaps because of differences in the climate, this is uncommon here so far, but if you do spot any cankerous growth on a pear, it should be cut back straight away. If you have this problem, the simplest way to solve it is to get rid of one of the plants. If I had a pear that was regularly producing succulent fruits, the juniper would get the chop, and I would kiss goodbye to any dreams I may have harboured of distilling my own gin and stick to pear cider instead. Unfortunately, the spores can travel three miles or more, so unless you know that no one in the vicinity has an avenue of junipers, you will need to be vigilant about this on your pears. If this causes a rust-war with your juniper-loving neighbours, pears trump junipers. Every time.

Other rusts

Orange to brown ferrous-looking patches appear mainly on leaves, sometimes on stems, seemingly at any time of year, and on almost any plant, though they are mostly prevalent in warm, damp weather, so common from late summer into autumn when humidity levels can be expected to rise. Rusts are caused by a number of fungi, attacking roses and other plants. As far as edible crops are concerned, it's your soft fruits that are most likely to succumb (but keep an eye on your mints as well) and there's no fungicide available, so look for varieties that have known resistance. None is truly immune but you can reduce the risk of infection by spacing vulnerable plants well for good air circulation. For ornamentals there may be a suitable fungicide, but check the label to see if the product is suitable for the plant you had in mind. Otherwise it's a matter of cutting off affected leaves and stems and consigning them to the bonfire or the household waste.

Hollyhocks are notoriously prone to rusts and many gardeners have given up on them for that very reason – but no self-styled cottage garden would be complete without them. Some newer varieties have a degree of resistance, but carefully check over the leaves of any young plants you are considering buying in a garden centre.

THE DOG DAYS OF SUMMER – DROUGHT

Everybody knows that plants go dormant in winter, many losing their leaves, others disappearing underground altogether (and some actually die, though that's another story). What's less widely appreciated is that they can also experience dormancy in summer, as when the temperature rises above a certain level, plant growth stops. That's not necessarily a bad thing, as everybody appreciates a good rest during a heatwave and, just like you, plants will benefit from a few weeks of doing nothing beyond soaking up the rays. There's no tanning lotion for plants, so as the sun beats down, the bark on your trees and shrubs turns leathery and thickens up and, as the soil dries out, roots reach down to whatever moisture remains well below the surface. So, at the end of a hot period, you have a plant with a tough outer bark and a deep root system that is well prepped to deal with savage winter frosts. That's the theory anyway, but if the temperature rises so high that plants start to suffer visibly, you may have a problem. Symptoms of drought are often easily mistaken for disease, and can indeed lead to disease, one of the consequences being powdery mildew. Worst case scenario: if an established tree or shrub suddenly loses all its leaves and looks dead, you

may find the cause is the dreaded honey fungus, of which you'll see an outward manifestation in autumn.

During periods of drought, leaves crisp up or shed prematurely, and flowers open and go over seemingly in minutes. If the plant is well established – three to five years old or more – it will probably be fine and this is simply its way of coping with stress. Most of your deciduous plants will experience drought as a kind of premature autumn, while your evergreens are more vulnerable but can usually recover quickly after a thorough drenching.

A dried-up lawn is nothing to worry about – let it turn brown, it will come to no harm and sprinkling is not necessary, both easing local demands on the water supply and saving you money. The first shower of rain following the drought will perk it up again, and you can deal with any remaining bald patches in autumn.

Drought is much more of an issue in the productive parts of the garden, particularly for fruit and leafy vegetables. Keep watering fruit bushes to keep the fruits plump and juicy, otherwise they will dry out and shrivel. Ideally, you will have planted your lettuces, spinach and other leafy crops somewhere shaded, but a daily watering is also beneficial. In all cases, thick mulches of straw can keep soil cool and moist around plant roots, but shouldn't lead to complacency. Lift the straw periodically to make sure the soil is still moist and water it if not.

If you are growing sweet peas for cut flowers, cut the flowers daily to prevent seed formation, which exhausts the plant and inhibits further flower production.

You can apply that principle to all your annuals as the flowers will start going to seed at a rate of knots in hot weather and you want them to keep on flowering.

As an aside, if you have large tubs and hanging baskets filled with summer bedding plants, they need far less water in

summer than you think – just enough to moisten
the topmost layer of compost is plenty, and baskets
shouldn't be watered till they drip. The plants don't need it
and you also won't risk running up a huge water bill.

Since it seems we have to get used to annual heatwaves,
the best policy is to focus on plants that will thrive in hot,
dry conditions. Make sure all your leafy salad crops stay
cool and in sunny spots consider majoring on tomatoes,
peppers and aubergines. In borders, Mediterranean plants
such as lavender, rosemary, sage and cistus – as well as
Mexican salvias – will revel in the heat.

Chapter 5

AUTUMN

In my neck of the woods, you can tell it's autumn not so much by the mists and mellow fruitfulness as by the seemingly constant racket of chainsaws, hedge trimmers, strimmers and leaf blowers whose operators emerge from their sheds and garages as from a chrysalis. This seems to start just before the clocks go back, to be followed by bonfires.

There are certain home owners for whom gardening could be characterized as housework outdoors, and who want to make sure the garden looks neat and tidy over winter. All gardens tend to develop a raddled look from late summer onwards when a lot of plant material starts to fade from a combination of age and exhaustion and, to compound the problem, there's probably a lot of dense growth. As the temperature cools, moisture in the air condenses on the plants and, in combination with poor air circulation, opens the door to a multitude of fungal diseases. But before you reach for the power tools and shear everything back, spare a thought for the implications of this.

THE AUTUMN CLEAR-UP – IS IT WORTH IT?

Current thinking holds that excessive tidiness should be sacrificed for the benefit of the ecosystem overall – a strategy that suits lazy gardeners like me. Not only do seeds and berries feed birds and little furry creatures, but dead stems and plant detritus lying on the ground are home to a wide range of invertebrates and microscopic organisms. It's generally only in the productive part of the garden that you need to consider a clear-up, and that's only if you've had a problem during the preceding spring and summer. If you've identified those pests or diseases as the type that can survive in the soil long term, there's a strong argument for growing a different type of crop there the following year.

If you want to drastically cut back overgrown shrubs, leave it till those crisp sunny days of early January when everything has had a good rest. If you are really looking for a job to do in autumn, sort out that lawn.

Most insect pests have done their business during spring and summer and have scattered their eggs and pupae around the garden in readiness for next year, but there are a couple that suddenly get active just when you think you can't possibly have any more problems. Apart from these, autumn, when the curiously comforting smell of rotting wood pervades the air, is the season of fungi.

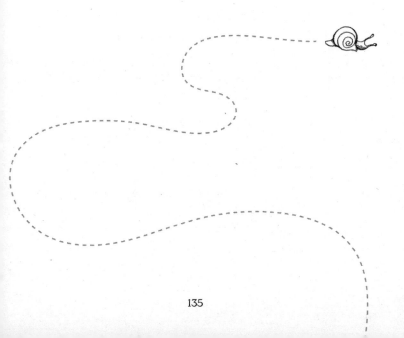

Spiders

Nobody seriously thinks that spiders are a pest, but many people have an aversion to them, at least in the house. They're especially active during autumn, their breeding period, and this is when you're likeliest to find them indoors. It's easy enough to trap them and move them outside, where they'll prey on any number of insects, including some pests. If you want to keep them happy outdoors, liberally mulch your borders with dry, loose material such as woodchips, straw, grass clippings or fallen leaves that give them shelter – another argument against an autumn clear-up. They are also partial to piles of logs (as are the equally desirable stag beetles), and nice tall perennials and shrubs that they can practise their climbing skills on (so again, don't cut these back in autumn). If you notice that single stemmed plants such as tomatoes, sweetcorn and sunflowers are festooned with their webs, take great care not to dislodge them when watering. If the weather's dry, put out a shallow dish of water in case they get thirsty.

LAWNS AND THEIR PROBLEMS

Many gardeners have an obsession with their lawns, and there's a whole industry devoted to encouraging it. As in other areas of the garden, a more casual approach will appeal to beneficial wildlife, and a less frequently mown lawn studded with daisies, clover, buttercups and even the odd dandelion can be a heart-gladdening sight. Even if you must have a neat lawn, it's a good idea to allow a few patches to grow unchallenged, or be mown less closely, or you could go for a sort of fade as offered by hipster barbers. You can have issues with the lawn at any time of year, but autumn is a great time for minimizing the chances of them recurring next year. Nearly all lawn problems not attributable to a specific pest or disease are down to poor drainage, or are directly caused by drought or waterlogging.

A gradually deteriorating lawn presents something of a vicious cycle. Whenever you mow, a certain amount of grass

clippings are left around the individual blades. Over time, these accumulate and create a mulch that prevents rainfall from washing down into the soil, starving the roots of moisture. To compound the issue, heavy use in summer can compact the ground so that rainfall can't penetrate, and bald patches appear. That in turn leads to the puddles you sometimes see on a lawn after a deluge. Summer drought can also lead to bald patches.

Whether you have an identifiable drainage problem or not, on a nice day in September or October you should rake the lawn to collect whatever dead plant material (known as 'thatch') has accumulated around the blades of grass at soil level. There will be more than you imagine. Proper lawn rakes with long, flexible tines that are curved at the tip are the tool of choice, but an ordinary rake can be just as effective, and you'll be glad you only need to do this once a year as, aside from the tedium, it's back breaking in the extreme. The next step is to fork all over the lawn to aerate it, just like when you do a blind bake. You can then top-dress with lawn sand. For any bald patches, fork over the soil with a hand fork, then reseed. Theoretically, you could do any of this in spring, but in practice there are enough other things to be getting on with then and, if you do it in autumn, the feeling of cosy complacency can sustain you through the winter.

One of the most intriguing lawn problems seen at this

time of year is the gelatinous patch, most likely to appear in damp, shady areas as the weather cools down, and caused by a primitive organism that isn't quite a bacterium – a real slipping hazard if not dealt with. If the shade is cast by an overhanging tree or shrub, you may find the jelly where rainwater has dripped from around the perimeter of the leaf canopy, so cut back any overhanging stems to admit more light to the grass. Other issues are lichens and algae that cause dark green or blackish patches on the lawn. There's no way of treating any of these other than to brush them off with a stiff, twiggy broom, of the type favoured by witches, then improve the drainage as described above.

Bleached patches on a lawn in late summer or autumn that then develop a pinkish tinge are evidence of red thread, a fungus that attacks starved grass. This is nothing to worry about, as lawn fertilizer the following spring should eliminate it.

If it's a particularly wet autumn and you manage to sort out your drainage problems, this may well lead to problems with leatherjackets the following spring, but at least you'll know to look out for these. If the lawn is ripped up by foxes, badgers or birds in autumn, these may not be your immediate problem. They are probably digging up succulent chafer grubs, if you didn't manage to deal with them in summer. Moles are active year round, but tend to be busiest in late

winter and early spring, depositing mounds of excavated soil all over the lawn surface.

Many fungi produce their fruiting bodies – mushrooms and toadstools – in autumn, and among the most intriguing are those that appear in rings on the lawn, 'fairy rings', to give them their Tolkienesque name. They can be tolerated unless parts of the lawn start to die off due to the underground parts of the fungus, the mycelium. This forms a mat that repels water so the grass roots dry off and the grass dies. You can dig out the ring to prevent further spread, but you have to dig to a depth of at least 30 cm, replace all the soil and reseed or returf. Much easier, given there are no reliable fungicides for this, to fork over any dead patches of turf to break up the mycelium, then reseed.

A lawn can be high maintenance at the best of times, so you may decide to dispense with one altogether, particularly if space is limited. An area of hard landscaping with plenty of containers can be more practical in an urban setting.

AUTUMN PESTS

Rosemary beetle

This is another pesky interloper unknown to our grandparents, infiltrating the UK from the South-East outwards. It seeks out rosemary and other aromatics such as lavender and sage, and breeds in late August and September, carrying on over winter (during mild weather) and into spring. Both adults and larvae, which pupate in the soil around the plants, feed on shoot tips and flowers. Close inspection and picking off the pests is the way to go and while extensive damage to plants is unlikely, you should still inform the RHS if you have an infestation, as they are tracking its progress.

Vine weevil

Adult vine weevils can't fly, but they are brilliant at parkour. Dark blackish brown, you're more likely to identify them from the damage caused by their revolting offspring. Notches eaten in the edges of leaves from August into September indicate that the adults are active and breeding and this is when you must make a pre-emptive strike against the larvae.

The adults like to clamber up the sides of greenhouses to reach the open vents, from which they drop down to the staging below. There they lay their eggs on the compost surface of potted plants, being especially fond of begonias. The hatchlings burrow downwards, then feast on the tuber. As this coincides with the point in the begonia's growth cycle when the top growth is dying back, you're often unaware there's a problem until the end of winter when it's time to coax the tubers back into life. Knock out the old compost at this time (February to March) and you'll see most of the tuber has been eaten and the old compost is full of fat white C-shaped grubs.

Hence, the time to deal with this pest is in autumn just after the eggs have hatched and before they start work in earnest. Keeping the greenhouse vents closed when the adults are laying towards the end of summer is not an option, as you need the ventilation to prevent overheating, stagnant air and the contingent proliferation of red spider mite. (As so often in gardening, you really cannot win.) There's a parasitic nematode you can buy via mail order which you can water into the compost, and this is highly effective. Otherwise, it's a matter of getting all the plants out of their pots, removing all the old compost and washing the roots thoroughly under running water to flush out any eggs and hatchlings, then repotting in fresh compost.

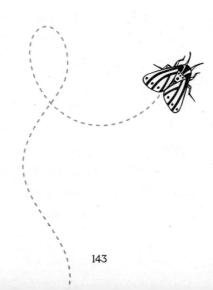

AUTUMN DISEASES

Botrytis

Rather like the common cold, botrytis, sometimes referred to as grey mould, is virtually unavoidable. It thrives in the same sort of conditions as downy mildew (which you also need to keep a lookout for at this time of year), but is caused by a different range of pathogens. The symptoms are unmistakable, a grey, fuzzy bum fluff that appears on leaves and stems mainly in autumn, though some summer soft fruits can also be affected. On strawberries, you can neatly reduce the risk of it spreading by putting dry straw around the plants on which the fruits can rest, well separated – possibly how they got their name.

Though it often strikes in spring, causing damping off of seedlings, it's usually worse towards the end of the year when, after a season's worth of growth, plants are crowded and congested, and, in many cases, starting to wither and die off. The disease takes hold during cool, damp weather, of the type commonly occurring at both ends of the growing season, particularly if the air is still. While the *laissez-faire* type of gardener would be happy to leave well alone 'for the wildlife', the garden hygienists whose urge is to cut back and burn any affected material may well have a point in this instance. Eco-warriors can counter that this doesn't solve the problem in the longer term, since botrytis spores are always in the air, so you are only removing the manifestations of their presence.

Botrytis can be a particular problem in greenhouses where, as you often need to keep the vents closed overnight in autumn to avoid too steep a drop in temperature, the air stagnates and any moisture held in it condenses on plants. You can reduce the risk by avoiding both overwatering pots and overhead watering, the practice you applied in summer. There is only one reliable solution: at the end of the season, reach for the disinfectant and give all the staging and pots a good scrub.

Bracket fungus

The clue's in the name: bracket fungi stick out from a tree trunk like wall-mounted shelves, usually quite low down but sometimes even into the crown. You can come across them at all times of year, but especially in autumn – and they can be beautiful, with an art nouveau colour palette.

Sometimes they're of little significance, but since they mainly appear on mature trees, they can affect their stability as they eat into the trunk's tissues. Even if the tree doesn't keel over, branches can be shed. Removal of the brackets might give temporary respite but doesn't cure the problem, so you really need to call in a professional arboriculturist for advice, the sort with letters after their name, not some random with a chainsaw. Any tree surgery required needs to be carefully done to maintain the balance of the tree.

The dreaded honey fungus

Hopefully, this is something you'll never encounter as, if you do, the remedy is drastic. Fungi are primary decomposers of wood, essential in any balanced ecosystem, so can often be tolerated. Unfortunately, this one pursues a policy of annihilation, killing almost any plant in its path, especially apple trees. The tree will look ill, and there'll be no mistaking. Most woody plants can survive a summer drought by shedding a proportion of their leaves, but if whole branches actually die, check for tell-tale signs of honey fungus in autumn.

You may notice a cluster of honey-coloured toadstools springing up at the base of the tree at this time of year, but this isn't a given. If you suspect you have honey fungus, peel back the bark just above ground level to expose the cambium and a film of white fungal tissue is a sure indicator. The fungus also produces black, bootlace-like threads underground (rhizomorphs), but these can be harder to identify as they are well camouflaged.

There's no chemical control. To eradicate the disease, you'll have to dig out the tree and its roots and burn them, a job for a professional. That will destroy the fungus's food source, but there's always the danger that any remaining rhizomorphs in the soil will set off in search of other plant roots to latch on to. To prevent this, surround the area the excavated tree occupied with a strip of impermeable pond liner, to a depth of 45 cm. Replacing the soil within the bounds of the liner before replanting wouldn't be a bad idea, or you could replant the area with plants that are known to have some resistance to the fungus.

Just pray it never happens to you. As a ray of hope, there's evidence that mycorrhizal fungi can outcompete honey fungus and thus restrict its spread. These fungi, often used by rose growers to help plants establish quickly, can be used for all woody plants. If you use them routinely when planting, you may never have to face the possibility of honey fungus.

Peach leaf curl

It might seem perverse to put this problem in autumn when it's down to a fungus that affects the young leaves in spring, but if you are determined to grow this most demanding fruit, autumn is when you need to take preventive action, the only means of control. This disease is well nigh impossible to halt in its tracks and is one of the most heartbreaking of all garden problems. Some gardeners have given up on growing peaches precisely for this reason as there is no reliable fungicide to deal with it.

Peaches, though perfectly hardy, are usually trained against a warm wall in the UK climate, necessary to shelter the early blossom from winter frost and to provide additional heat to ripen the fruits in summer. The leaves appear after the blossom, a delicious bright, soft green. Then you notice a couple are puckered and twisted. Once you start removing these, as you should, you will gradually realise that practically the whole tree is affected. If you choose to leave them on, they will fall to the ground of their own accord and the disease will persist in the soil to affect the tree the following year. Peach leaf curl isn't a killer, but it weakens the tree, which has to put its energies into producing a fresh crop of leaves rather than developing fruits.

The fungus is carried in rainfall and, in the absence of a fungicide, your only option in guarding against the disease is a physical barrier. Screen the whole plant with a sheet of clear plastic, stretched from the top of the wall to the ground, secured in place around 30 cm from the wall. The screen needs to be open at both ends to allow free passage of air around the plant and to let in pollinating insects when the flowers open in late winter. (As a bonus, it protects the blossom from those pesky bullfinches.)

Rose-sick soil/replant disease

Old-school gardeners will assure you that rose-sick soil is an actual thing. Others, myself included, have been sceptical, but recent research suggests that the oldies were right all along.

Autumn is the best time for planting roses, giving them plenty of time to get their roots down before spring. Conventional wisdom has always been, however, that you should not plant a new rose in soil in which a rose has already been growing, as the previous rose will have sucked out all the nutrients in the soil. If the rose was there since the 1970s and has been neglected, this may well be the case. But if it was nurtured, fed, mulched and watered as appropriate, there should be no issue: the soil should still be in good enough heart to sustain the newcomer. That's been the argument I've been using hitherto.

Nowadays, it's thought that to make any new rose thrive, whether it's replacing an earlier rose or not, mycorrhizal fungi should be added to the base of the planting hole. These fungi, processed as a dry compound, are widely available from commercial rose growers and in garden centres. In contact with moisture around the roots, they reactivate and effectively create a secondary root system that delivers extra water to the plant. (The fungi can be used when planting any woody plant, not just roses.)

Recent research, however, suggests that there are certain pathogens in the soil that the previous rose had built immunity to over time but that may attack the younger, finer roots of the replacement, irrespective of whether the soil is well maintained and your use of the fungi. There's a way of combatting these pathogens, but you do need to plan ahead. After removing the old rose in spring, sow French marigolds, specifically the variety 'Nema'. In autumn, dig these into the soil. Apparently, this boosts the nematode content of the soil which can help reduce the impact of the pathogens.

Still with me? The following spring, dig a hole for the new rose large enough to accommodate a cardboard wine box (or other cardboard box of similar size). Plant the rose in the box and fill it with soil from another part of the garden which has never had roses growing in it, ideally enriched with fresh compost. By the time the roots have grown sufficiently to penetrate the disintegrating box, they should be established enough to withstand any remaining nasties in the soil.

Frankly, the business with the marigolds strikes me as a step too far for most gardeners, especially those who aren't willing to hang about and lose a whole year without a rose, though I don't doubt the research. So do your planting in autumn. Just dig up the old rose, excavate the soil to accommodate the new one in its box, and you should have no problems.

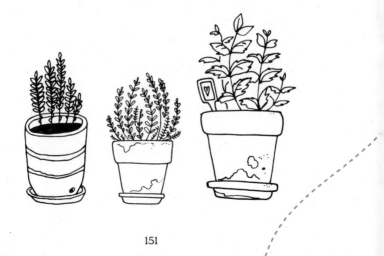

NOT SO MELLOW FRUITFULNESS

Trees give a garden an air of permanence. But fruit trees can sometimes disappoint, failing to achieve their potential, usually as a result of adverse weather conditions. There's often not a lot you can do, but for specific issues you can take preventive measures.

Biennial bearing

Biennial bearing is a strange but common problem of apples (and a few pears), some varieties being more prone than others. The tree crops prolifically one year to the point of exhaustion, so it requires a kind of gap year to recover, when it produces barely any fruit at all. This habit becomes ingrained, causing on–off years in perpetuity.

The initial cause may be any number of factors, but a sudden cold spell or pest attack around flowering time can set it off. If all the blossom is killed there'll be no crop that year, and the tree will make up for it by flowering profusely the year following, something to note on the spreadsheet. Alternatively, a hot summer followed by a cold winter can make a tree flower to the point of exhaustion. Plums occasionally do the same thing, to the extent that in a heavy-cropping season the volume of fruit will weigh down the branches and tear them from the trunk. Fruit thinning is essential to avoid this and can also reduce the risk of gumming in summer.

Apples routinely shed a proportion of their fruits in early summer anyway – the so-called June drop. If the remaining crop is a heavy one, pick off a proportion of the fruits to leave a well-spaced crop – they should be about 10–15 cm apart, more if it's a large-fruited variety such as a Bramley. Alternatively, you could thin the blossom in spring, removing some clusters entirely, then reducing the number of blossoms within each remaining cluster.

For sheer tedium, this is the worst job in the gardening year.

Bitter pit (apples)

Almost everyone who grows apples has come across this problem. It is easily fixed, in principle, though it can be heavy work. Bitter pit looks like a horrible disease, but it's not actually caused by a pathogen. So what is it? Around harvest time, you'll notice that fruits (possibly nearly all of them) are spotted with dark brown within and have a bitter taste, if you try eating one. Annoyingly, affected fruits that present as perfect to all outward appearances can deteriorate in storage till they're inedible. If a cooking apple is only lightly affected you can still use it, but may need more sugar than usual to disguise the nasty taste. The cause is lack of water during fruit development, typically caused by a prolonged period of summer drought, which prevents the tree from taking on board adequate amounts of calcium.

Some varieties are more susceptible than others, Bramleys and Coxes being particularly at risk. The simplest way of avoiding the problem is to give trees a good drenching in summer, if the weather won't oblige (and you'll need bucketloads). Very established trees may be OK without this as their deep roots can take up whatever moisture remains in the soil, but young trees may need all the extra water you can provide. Hold back on the fertilizers at this time (assuming you were so minded) and carry out a light prune, trimming back any new growth that's shading the fruits. This will not only help them ripen in the sun but divert what moisture there is into them.

If you are really determined to get on top of the problem, you can spray trees from mid-June to mid-September with a solution of calcium nitrate.

A similar issue can affect your tomatoes.

Poor fruit set

Many fruit trees – some apples, some plums, most pears and cherries – need a so-called compatible pollinator in the vicinity for good fruiting, so if you consistently fail to get a reliable crop on your plants, it may be that speed dating is required. Plenty of people have an apple tree in their garden and chance seedlings appear in many a hedgerow, so this is not usually a problem. Fewer grow pears and cherries. Several varieties are known to be self-fertile, but even these can crop better with a compatible pollinator.

Environmental factors can also play a role. The tree may flower prolifically, but a sudden late frost overnight can kill the blossom so no fruits are set. Equally, a spell of miserable weather at flowering time will put all the pollinators off (they may not emerge from their hibernation to do their work) or, as commonly happens with grapes, prevent the flowers from forming properly in the first place.

While there's little you can do in the short term, a poor crop one year can flip a fruit tree into the biennial bearing habit – especially for some apple and plum varieties.

If you're shopping for new fruit trees, check the flowering time, if you can. Those that flower later in spring, when the flowers are less likely to succumb to frost, are generally a safer bet if you're in a chilly part of the country (though there are

never any guarantees). And plant plenty of spring bulbs and early-flowering perennials such as hellebores and fragrant wallflowers that are known to attract pollinating insects into the garden.

Chapter 6

WINTER

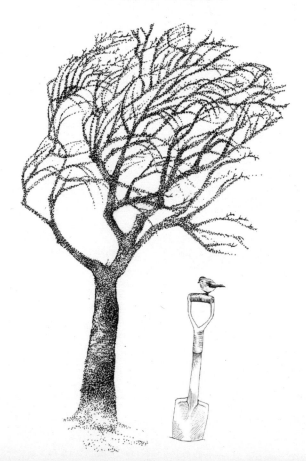

Winter is largely a time for hunkering down and leaving the garden alone. Apart from the annuals that have died, plants are having a good rest and you, probably needing it even more, can put your feet up with a clear conscience. Gardeners are great at putting the disasters of the previous seasons behind them and planning for the future as if none of them happened, but there are a few issues you need to tackle now for complete peace of mind.

The best way to beat those post-Christmas blues is to get out into the garden, particularly after a cold snap. Freezing temperatures will kill many of last year's harmful bacteria and fungi that may be lurking at ground level as well as some pests (including pupae and eggs) that were in a state of dormancy. This would be a good time for that clear-up you were itching to do in autumn, to make way for all the spring problems to come.

JACK FROST AND THE SNOW QUEEN

You are likely to see more of the former than the latter, though neither is welcome as cold weather can kill even hardy plants. Your evergreen shrubs can be vulnerable, particularly bay trees, ceanothus (the deciduous ones are generally tougher) and pittosporums. A little wilting at the ends of stems is tolerable, but browning leaves can be serious. Later in winter, shear back to where you can feel swellings in the stems – dormant buds that will repair the damage – or wait till the equinox for signs of new growth. Young and newly planted specimens that have yet to get their roots down are more vulnerable, so it is worth tenting these with horticultural fleece or even newspaper, which you can attach to the stems with clothes pegs whenever a hard frost is forecast. If you're handy with a sewing machine (or staple gun), you could make bespoke bags for each plant. Keep your eye also on young hedging plants, particularly of the coniferous variety, which can easily frazzle at low temperatures, if they're not killed outright.

TV gardeners love to show you how to pack up your banana palms with straw and chicken wire over winter but, more generally, dry straw is great for packing around the base of any vulnerable plant, including your dahlias if you've decided to risk leaving them in the ground over winter. Many plants with top growth damaged by frost can regenerate, provided the soil is kept from freezing around their roots. There aren't many evergreen perennials, but you can expect the few there are, particularly hellebores and bergenias, to look the worse for wear over winter. This is nothing to worry about, but you can cut back any blackened or ragged-looking leaves in January, as they might introduce disease in the plant as they decay.

If you've planted early potatoes, late frosts can cause a collapse of their foliage. You can avoid this by covering them loosely with horticultural fleece, held down at the edges with heavy stones or bricks. If it's a prolonged cold snap, you can leave this on in the daytime – the plants won't be growing if it's too cold, so you won't be stunting them. They'll soon perk up once the temperature rises.

Nearly all plants emerge unscathed from a blanket of snow, even the sweet pea seedlings that I now prefer to sow in pots outdoors in October (much easier to manage than spring sowings). Large shrubs and conifers can be bent out of shape by a heavy snowfall but I have never known them not return to form once the snow has gone (you can brush it off, if you prefer). In the event that the weight of the snow breaks the stems, cut them back on the first clear, dry day that follows.

Crop rotation – is it worth it?

Many gardeners start planning the following year's crops in winter, so this is a good time to take stock of the previous year's calamities and decide what you can do to limit the damage next year.

Any old gardening manual is likely to extol the benefits of crop rotation. To avoid a build-up of nasties in the soil, different crops are grown in clearly delineated areas of the plot on a three- or four-year cycle. The pathogen that causes clubroot on your cabbages in summer, for example, can build up to the extent that certain crops become ungrowable.

Done correctly, crop rotation involves a knowledge of plant families and flair for forward planning and record keeping that are frankly beyond me and may bring significant dividends only on a small-holding or a large plot. In the average domestic garden, rotating crops will have only a limited impact as pests and diseases can spread easily within such a small area. Rotation is sometimes necessary to prevent specific issues, especially those concerning potatoes, but a more practical policy for good crops is to keep the soil fertile with regular additions of organic material that help keep down disease. Intercropping, whereby different crops are grown in close proximity to attract a range of insect predators, is also effective.

OTHER WINTER PROBLEMS

The little foxes

These urbanistas are seemingly out on the razz every night of the week, lurking around the dustbins at your front gate like drug-dealers looking for trade. To many gardeners, they are the devil incarnate, digging up plants, chewing through hosepipes, ripping up grass or marking their territory with deposits of pungent material that your dog will love to roll in. Foxes are active throughout the year, but during the winter mating season they screech at each other for attention.

Foxes need to be managed rather than controlled. Repellants, including the ultrasonic types, are unlikely to be effective, and you won't easily keep them out with fencing, as you might do for rabbits. Lock any animal-based fertilizers such as chicken manure and bonemeal in the garage if possible, as they are drawn by the scent. If you find any holes they've dug in the garden, you know they're casing the joint with their eye on their forever home. Fill them in before they can establish a den or you will have the (undeniably cute) cubs to manage the following summer.

You'll find all kinds of advice online about how to deal with them, but I would be reluctant to use night lighting as a deterrent. Effective though this might be, it would also put off any bats and spiders that help control invertebrate pests, not to mention annoying the neighbours.

Moles

The hillocks of soil moles deposit on the surface of a lawn quite ruin it. Their tunnelling can also damage plant roots elsewhere in the garden, but they don't actually eat plants, unlike insect pests, and they tend to be solitary and territorial, so although the damage might look extensive, you usually have only one culprit to deal with. As miners, they can also cause subsidence, and you may find the ground suddenly giving way under your feet, so you lose your footing and potentially twist your ankle.

Ultrasound can drive a mole away, though this may be temporary, or the mole might ignore it. You could hire a pest control company but, assuming you're not work shy, the humane option is to dig up the whole lawn (yes, really), peg down anti-mole netting, a tough plastic mesh sold on the roll, over the whole area, then replace the lawn. You'll find you can dig up the turf quite readily, stack it neatly, then relay it. A great job for a sunny weekend after Christmas.

Rabbits, hares and deer

These can be lumped together, attractive creatures that nevertheless cause havoc in the garden. They are active all year round, but it's often in winter that they cause unexpected, and sometimes quite serious, damage.

Rabbits are the commonest. They love all soft new growth in spring but in winter, when food is scarce, they'll rip the bark off trees and shrubs, opening them up to disease and potentially killing them if they manage to gnaw their way round the whole circumference of the trunk. If only part of the bark has been stripped away, cover the exposed area with black plastic to prevent water getting in and compounding the risk of rotting.

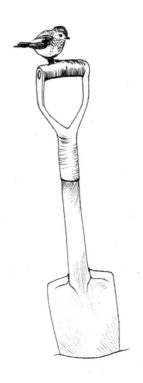

Physical barriers are the best way to deter bunnies. You can save young trees from being attacked in winter by wrapping expandable tree guards around the lower section of trunk, but for a garden-wide solution you need a pest-proof fence. This needs to be sunk 30 cm into the ground to prevent them tunnelling in, with a height at least a metre above the ground. During the growing season, protect individual plants such as lilies by surrounding them with a column of wire netting – unsightly but effective. You can buy chemical repellants for spraying on plants but these need replacing regularly, especially in wet weather. Be particularly cautious if you are applying these to edible plants and certainly desist near harvest time, or the crop will taste as disgusting to you as it does to the rabbits.

Hares add greatly to the gaiety of the nation: treat as for rabbits.

During Covid lockdown, many town-dwellers were alternately shocked and delighted to find deer wandering through the deserted streets, but urban populations have been on the increase for at least the last decade. Deer will graze your plants at ground level and browse them at head height. Like rabbits, they'll eat tree bark in winter. Unlike rabbits, however, they won't burrow their way in – but will need a fence at least 2 m high to keep them out. Again, repellant sprays will be of short-term effectiveness only.

Winter moth

This is one of the few invertebrate pests that is active in winter. While it's the caterpillars that cause all the damage, and these can be dealt with by an insecticide in spring, it's more eco-friendly to use a barrier method that prevents the adults from laying their eggs in the first place.

Only the males look like regular moths, and you may catch them in your car headlights flitting through the hedgerows as you drive down country lanes of a winter's evening. Female winter moths have no wings, so have to leg it everywhere. Having pupated at the base of a tree over summer, they shimmy up the trunk, wafting pheromones that lure in any passing swains, then lay their eggs in the branches or in cracks in the bark any time from November to April. The simplest control method is to wrap a sticky grease band around the trunk in late autumn to stop them in their tracks. Don't be tempted to use strong glue as an alternative as this can trap beneficials, even small birds and bats.

When all's said and done, it's only your fruit trees that need protecting from this pest, and any damage the caterpillars inflict is likely to affect just a small proportion of the fruits. If you didn't manage to girdle your trees in winter, before reaching for the chemical sprays in spring, spare a thought for the nesting birds that rely on the caterpillars as a food source for their little ones. We should cherish moths as much as butterflies, and since there are precious few about in winter, this one clearly makes a valuable contribution to the ecosystem.

Storage rots

A shed or garage stacked with lovingly harvested crops of root vegetables can see you through winter, so it is heartbreaking to find them rotting off. Fungal and bacterial infections can also affect stored fruits and dahlia and begonia tubers. As these are often caused by pathogens that were present in the crop, which then develop and spread in storage, store only firm, perfect crops in the first place. However, some outwardly perfect produce may also harbour the disease. Damp, stagnant air can be a killer, so keep your storage areas well ventilated.

Affected crops soften and probably show signs of fungus on the skin. Since this can spread rapidly, you need to check everything in storage frequently so you can remove any suspect item.

GETTING AHEAD OF NEXT YEAR'S PROBLEMS

In an ideal world, you'd never have to deal with any gardening issue more than once, as second time round you'd know what to do. Gardening's never quite like that, of course, but you'd prefer not to be fighting the same battles in perpetuity. It would be worth compiling a list of all the things that would have come in handy over the year – not just pesticides, fungicides and repellants, but horticultural fleeces, netting and cloches – so you'll have them to hand at the first hint of a problem. You can light up any gardener's face on

Christmas Day by giving them a bag of grit, essential for adding to compost for seed sowing to improve drainage and eliminate spring-time stress about damping off. It can also be

sprinkled over the compost surface of your potted plants to avoid waterlogging later on.

I find it difficult to be sentimental about mice, which will nibble at all your crops and bulbs in store and any late winter sowings. Set a few mouse traps or lay down poison if you see any evidence of these rodents in the greenhouse, garage, shed, or house. They don't hibernate and may well be active in spells of mild weather. Get on top of them now so you won't have hordes of them to deal with in summer. Personally, I don't see the 'humanity' in incarcerating them live, then releasing them in the wild some miles distant.

That strategy must surely send their stress levels soaring and they may well meet a grisly death in the jaws of a predator following their bewildered release. A swift despatch at home may actually be kinder. Few of us have any compunction about murdering rats.

Mild, damp winters, when many pests and diseases pull through to strike again, are a gardener's bugbear. Loath as I am to indulge in an autumn clear-up, some clearing of the decks in late winter is worth it in the veg garden to get rid of any overwintering pupae and eggs, especially if there was no heavy frost or snowfall that would have done some of the work for you. Washing your pots and seed trays to get rid of any fungal spores or pest eggs prior to seed sowing is a thankless, if necessary, task.

Fungicidal washes over your fruit bushes, roses and other plants as early as January – especially if it was a damp autumn – can kill overwintering fungal spores so long as you factor in that a fresh wave of fungi will arrive in spring rainfall. Doing any winter pruning during a spell of dry weather will allow wounds to callus over properly before they get wet in the next shower, otherwise disease can enter through the cuts.

Assuming you managed to keep a gardening diary or spreadsheet over the course of the year, now would be a good time to review it and think about a timetable for seed sowing and planting out so as to avoid the periods when pests and diseases are most likely. The vagaries of British weather can scupper even the most carefully laid plans, so be prepared to make adjustments as you go and have your armoury of choice (be it pesticides, fungicides or simple barriers) at the ready.

Your new year's resolution needs to be – start that slug control early.

GLOSSARY

Acid Of soil, having a pH below 7; so-called ericaceous (acid-loving) plants need acid soil or compost.

Alkaline Of soil, having a pH above 7; the alkalinity of the soil can be raised by additions of lime.

Annual A plant that germinates, flowers, sets seed and dies within a calendar year.

Biennial bearing Of a fruit tree, producing a heavy crop one year with a much lighter crop the year following to compensate.

Biological control A method of controlling pests by introducing their natural predators into the environment.

Cambium The layer of tissue on a woody plant that lies just below the bark.

Canker An area of dead tissue, usually on a woody plant and caused by a fungus, bacterium or virus.

Chlorosis A yellowing of plant leaves usually caused by a nutrient deficiency, but sometimes by pests or diseases.

Cocoon, *see* **Pupa**

Compost 1. Made in a compost heap, comprising broken-down organic matter such as vegetable waste possibly with additions of animal manure. 2. A bagged, sterilized product, intended for growing plants in containers and raising seedlings; seed composts have a fine texture and low fertility; ericaceous composts are used for acid-loving plants.

Crop rotation A system historically used in vegetable gardens where different crops are grown annually in clearly delineated parts of the plot, usually on a four- or five-year cycle.

Damping off The collapse of seedlings grown in containers resulting from a fungal infection.

Deciduous Of a plant, losing its leaves in winter.

Eelworm, *see* **Nematode**

Evergreen Of a plant, retaining its leaves in winter.

Fertilizer An organic or inorganic compound, usually in powdered, granular or liquid form, applied to plants to boost growth and improve flowering and fruiting. Products high in nitrogen (N) promote leafy growth in spring; those high in potassium (K), such as most tomato and rose fertilizers, encourage flower and fruit formation.

Fleece, *see* **Horticultural fleece**

Fruiting body Of a fungus, the spore-bearing part of the organism that appears above ground, often as a toadstool or mushroom.

Fungicide A chemical product formulated to kill fungi.

Gall A woody protuberance on a plant usually caused by a bacterium.

Green manure A non-edible crop sown on bare soil, usually during winter, that is then dug into the soil to improve its fertility.

Gumming A sticky, resin-like substance seen on tree trunks, branches and fruits (often on plum trees); generally caused by lack of water or other environmental factors.

Honeydew A sticky, shiny deposit on the upper surfaces of leaves produced by aphids, scale insects and other invertebrate pests.

Horticultural fleece A thin material, usually a synthetic, that can be spread over plants directly or suspended over them on a framework to protect them from frost and/or certain invertebrate pests.

Insecticide A chemical product formulated to kill insect pests.

Intercropping The mixing of different crops together in a bed, sometimes alongside ornamentals.

Larva (pl. larvae) A caterpillar, maggot or grub, the juvenile stage of a usually flighted insect such as a butterfly, moth or fly.

Leafhopper A sap-sucking insect that jumps or flies; many leafhoppers are harmless but they can spread disease through their mouth parts.

Legume Podded vegetables such as peas and beans and some ornamentals, such as sweet peas and wisteria.

Lime A compound present in the soil, amounts of which determine whether it is acid, alkaline or neutral.

Mildew A type of fungus or mould often seen on leaf surfaces.

Mulch A layer of material, usually organic, spread on the soil surface around plants to improve soil structure and fertility and retain soil moisture around the roots.

Mycelium The thread-like structure (often, though not always, underground) of a fungus, that plays an important part in the decomposition of plant material.

Mycorrhizal fungi Beneficial fungi that attach themselves to the roots of mainly woody plants, creating a secondary root system.

Nematode A microscopic worm-like organism that lives in the soil; nematodes are also known as eelworms. Most are benign, but some can damage plants; some are predatory and are used in biological control.

Organic Of a product, derived from naturally occurring compounds.

Pathogen A microorganism that causes disease.

Perennial A plant that lives for three or more years; usually applied to soft-stemmed ornamental plants.

Perlite Lightweight granules of expanded, volcanic glass, white in colour and usually added to potting compost to improve drainage. *See also* **Vermiculite**

Pesticide A chemical product formulated to kill pests.

Pheromone trap Used to trap the males of certain flighted pests by means of a sticky substance that mimics the scent of the females.

Pupa The resting stage of certain insect pests, during which time the larva metamorphoses into the adult form.

Repellant A product sprayed over plants or placed on the soil in their vicinity that deters pests either by its scent or taste; most need to be replaced regularly.

Rhizomorph The underground part of certain fungi (for instance honey fungus) that performs a similar function to plant roots.

Seed compost, *see under* **Compost**

Slime mould A composite organism involved in the decomposition of some plant material; sometimes seen on lawns.

Systemic Of a product, absorbed by the plant.

Tender perennial A perennial plant that cannot survive frosts. In mild areas, tender perennials may survive the winter outdoors, otherwise cuttings taken in September can be overwintered in frost-free conditions.

Tuber An underground storage organ of a plant, sometimes edible. Begonias and potatoes produce tubers.

Vermiculite A lightweight, biscuit-coloured mineral used to improve the drainage of potting compost. *See also* **Perlite**

Weevil A type of beetle with elongated mouth parts; many are serious plant pests.

ACKNOWLEDGEMENTS

This book would not exist without Nicki Crossley, the publisher who commissioned it, and who was unfailingly courteous throughout the process of its creation. I am grateful both to her and its editor, Gabby Nemeth, who did a very good job of neatly pruning into shape some garbled copy. Fay Martin's and Julyan Bayes' illustrations are a delight and a significant enhancement. I am also indebted to my friend and colleague Maria Summerscale, who kindly read through the text before I submitted it and made several helpful suggestions.

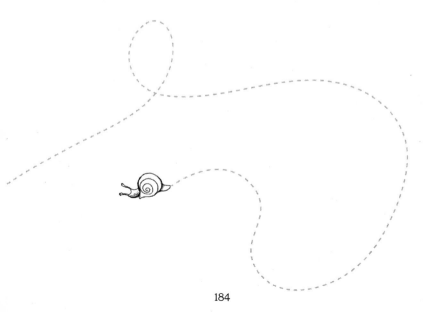

SOME USEFUL WEBSITES

We all rely on the internet for information, but be on guard when making searches. Many will lead you to American sites that deal with transatlantic pests and diseases and local control methods that may not be appropriate (or even legal) in the UK. Moreover, the wide climate range of that continent will give skewed information when it comes to the timing of pest activity and controls. The following are reliable resources for UK gardeners.

Royal Horticultural Society (RHS)

www.rhs.org.uk
My go-to resource. Easily searchable, it's regularly updated and pitched at UK gardeners just like you.

Pesticide Action Network (PAN)

pan-international.org
An international coalition that promotes alternatives to hazardous pesticides. Somewhat hardcore.

Neudorff

www.neudorff.co.uk
A German-based company that produces a range of chemicals for the amateur gardener.

Gardeners' World

www.gardenersworld.com

The digital arm of the popular BBC *Gardeners' World* magazine. Easily searchable.

The Woodland Trust

www.woodlandtrust.org.uk

A great resource for information on UK wildlife and nature conservation in general.

Vitax Ltd

www.vitax.co.uk

Trusted manufacturer of garden fertilizers, pesticides and pheromone traps.

Westland Horticulture Ltd

www.gardenhealth.com

Pest killers and repellants as well as protective fleeces, meshes and netting.

gardening-naturally

www.gardening-naturally.com

A range of environmentally friendly solutions, including biological controls.

INDEX

Index